THE CONTRACT WITH YOURSELF

TAKE BACK CONTROL of your life with the
most important contract you will ever need!

THE
CONTRACT
WITH
YOURSELF

DINESHRIE PILLAY

Quickfox

Published by Quickfox Publishing
PO Box 50660 West Beach 7449
Cape Town, South Africa
www.quickfox.co.za
info@quickfox.co.za

Available from:
www.dineshriepillay.com
www.publisher.co.za
And leading bookstores locally and internationally

The Contract With Yourself
ISBN 978-0-620-81735-6

Second edition 2018

Copyright © 2018 Dineshrie Pillay
www.dineshriepillay.com

All rights reserved. No part of this publication may be reproduced, stored in a retrieval system, or transmitted, in any form or by any means, without the prior written permission of the author.

Edited by Michelle Bovey-Wood
Proofread by Vanessa Wilson
Cover design by Leo Design Agency
Photography and cover profile picture by Brandon Barnard
Typesetting and production by Quickfox Publishing

This book is dedicated to my parents, for instilling within me, from a young age, the value of education.
Thank you for your unwavering support and belief in my abilities.
The contract with *myself* started many years ago – and it began with you.

Dineshrie

DISCLAIMER

The advice contained in this material might not be suitable for everyone. The author designed the information to present her opinion about the subject matter. The reader should carefully investigate all aspects of any decision before committing him or herself to any course of action.

The author compiled the information contained herein from various sources that she believes to be reliable, and from her own personal experience, but she neither implies nor intends any guarantee of accuracy. The author particularly disclaims any liability, loss or risk taken by persons who directly or indirectly act on the information contained herein. The author believes the advice presented here to be sound, but readers cannot hold her responsible for either the actions they take, or the results of those actions.

Foreword

> *When you are inspired by some great purpose, some extraordinary project, all your thoughts break their bonds, your mind transcends limitations, your consciousness expands in every direction, and you find yourself in a new, great, and wonderful world. Dormant forces, faculties, and talents become alive, and you discover yourself to be a greater person by far than you ever dreamed yourself to be.*
>
> **PATANJALI**

When I was a young girl, my parents encouraged me to focus on my education and learn to become independent. They would often remind me of the importance of achieving good grades in school and in university. Comic books were replaced with encyclopedias; excessive exposure to television was replaced with library cards that encouraged further reading and growth; and toys mainly took the form of educational games, puzzles and creative activities. Fun, entertainment and loads of laughter came in the form of my two brothers. Together, we would fight and play pranks on each other, laugh at each other's jokes and go out and have fun. As a family, we have always been there for each other to guide, encourage and support one another in our journey through life.

When I failed my qualifying examination to become a Chartered Accountant for the second year in a row, I began to realize that there is a strong correlation between our mindset and our success in life. I understood at a very early stage that in order to achieve big aspirations I had to first work on myself. It was during this time that I began to focus my research in this area to try to understand the factors that drive human behavior. I continue to be inspired by each new principle that I discover and its impact on people once fully implemented.

The many principles and stories I am about to share with you are principles that form a foundation for living a healthy and fulfilling life just by focusing on and honouring the most important person in your life – YOU!

My suggestion to you, as you read this book, is to read and digest one chapter at a time. Keep a diary or journal with you as you read and note down any action points or inspiring ideas that may come up for you. Take the time to complete the activities at the end of each chapter. Understand that many of the ideas contained in each chapter may be new to you, so when you first complete the self-review questions, you may not have implemented all the action steps. This is okay. Re-read the chapter and re-assess yourself again within the next month.

Just as with a contract of employment, when you first start working you do not know everything about that job within the first week or the first month. Similarly with this book, many of the concepts may be new to you. Give yourself permission and the time needed to learn and apply each skill within your life.

The first step is to develop awareness. The second step is to take action. It is for this reason that each chapter in the book is separated into two sections. The first section provides the content and principles to instill awareness; the second section contains activities that you can take action on. Success is about doing the simple things on a consistent basis. This book is a reminder of all those simple things.

You are holding this book in your hand for a reason. I believe that there are no coincidences in the world and this book has found its way to you for a reason.

My hope for you is that you will use this book to make quantum leaps in your personal and professional life as you continue to walk along your unique path and journey in life.

Dineshrie Pillay

Table of contents

Introduction 13

1 **C**ommitment 17

2 **O**bserve 69

3 **N**est 85

4 **T**actics 101

5 **R**e-enforcement 121

6 **O**pposition 143

7 **L**ife 157

Afterword 175

Notes 177

Meet the author 181

Introduction

> *When I thought I could not go on, I forced myself to keep going. My success is based on persistence, not luck.*
>
> **NORMAN LEAR**

Your interview with the mirror

We live in a frenetic world in which everything is due yesterday. With continued advances in technology; the streamlining of business processes; and greater demands being placed on a smaller group of individuals, it is no wonder that stress, burn-out and frequent illnesses prevail.

One moment we are ushering in a new year – the next, we are taking leave for the Easter holidays. Then before we know it, October has arrived and retail stores are starting to put up their Christmas decorations!

In our pursuit to increase our material wealth, purchase luxury comforts, spend time with family and friends, build our careers, and expand our businesses, the question remains: When do you set time aside to take care of the most important person in your life – you?

Legal contracts

At this point, I would like you to reflect on your life.
What was the first legal contract you signed?

When did you first sign it?
Was it for your first job?
Was it a contract for your new vehicle?
Was it a rental agreement, or bond for your first house?
Was it a rental agreement or bond for your business premises?
Maybe it was the legal contract you signed when you got married.

What do all these legal contracts have in common?
1. They clearly specify **how the relationship will be managed**.
2. They remind all parties about **their respective responsibilities**.
3. They are agreements that dictate how you **commit yourself to other people**.

How many legal contracts currently exist in your life?
- Five contracts?
- Between five and ten contracts?
- More than ten contracts?

If, like most people, you have more than five contracts, no wonder your life is passing you by. You are so busy ensuring you meet your obligations to other people that you forget, or simply have no time, to meet your own obligations.

As long as you are in a legal contract with someone else, you are not entirely in control of your own dreams.

Attempts at finding 'me-time'

While we are busy being a 'rat' in this race we call life, we try to create me-time in various ways – some good, and some not as good.
The good attempts at me-time include, but are not limited to:
1. Full-day spa treatments.
2. Going on shopping sprees.
3. Taking weekend breaks at local retreats.

4. Spending time with family and friends.
5. Reading books.
6. Socializing and going out to movies, music concerts, or theatre.
7. Cooking a favorite meal, or going to a favorite restaurant.

The not-so-good attempts at me-time include, but are not limited to:
1. Over-eating and over-drinking.
2. Driving under the influence of alcohol.
3. Partying and drinking the night away.
4. Skipping daily exercise to laze around at home and watch television.
5. Substituting a healthy diet with sweets, fatty and processed meals and fast foods.
6. Sleeping away your time.
7. Becoming addicted to drugs, alcohol, cigarettes and social media – among other things – as a means to 'escape' and feel happy.

It is no wonder then that, by the end of the year, most people have gained weight, picked up bad habits, or have even developed new addictions. Their new year resolutions involve trying to improve on the poor attempts at me-time of the previous year.

The contract with yourself

What if there was a contract that expressly stipulated how you should run your life? A contract that was designed by you, signed by you, and monitored by you. A contract that honored the wishes of the most important person in your life – You!

Join me on a journey as I explore within this book seven simple principles that you can easily implement to take C.O.N.T.R.O.L. of your life.

This agreement is, without doubt, the most important document you will sign – the contract with yourself.

ONE

CREATING AWARENESS
COMMITMENT

PART ONE

COMMITMENT TO YOURSELF

> *We do not serve the world or ourselves by 'playing small'.*
> **MARIANNE WILLIAMSON**

Commitment. What does the word mean to you? If asked to visually depict the word 'commitment', you may think of two people shaking hands or perhaps of something more symbolic, like a wedding ring.

According to the *Oxford English Dictionary*, commitment is a noun that means:

Dedication to a cause or activity;
A promise to do something.

It is for this reason that commitment is the first principle within this book. Your life is about you dedicating to a cause or activity. In order to fulfill this cause, you promise to do certain things.

So, if I had to visualize what the word 'commitment' means to me, I would picture a person placing their right hand over their heart. For me, a commitment is something that you pledge to yourself. Before you can commit to others, you first uphold your personal commitments. If you easily break commitments to yourself, why should anyone else trust that you will uphold your commitments to them? When you dedicate yourself to a cause or activity, you promise yourself that you will do what it takes to get something done. It does not matter how long it takes; completing the task means upholding your commitment.

Commitment is a decision that you take. Once you make that decision, you then need to take action. Now this sounds easy in principle, but we all know of many examples where people break their commitments – either with themselves or others. Why is this so?

One example of breaking a commitment relates to new year resolutions. Research by the University of Scranton in the US reveals that a mere 8% of people actually achieve their new year resolutions. Most people give up on their new year resolutions by the second week of February.

This startling statistic becomes very evident when you observe the number of people attending gym at the beginning of the year, and the dwindling number of people in the gym by mid-February to early March.

Another common scenario is when someone is advised to read a book that could potentially help them succeed in their chosen field of study. Below are a few variations of how people will act on such advice.
- Person A: Knows of a good book, but does not buy it.
- Person B: Knows of a good book and buys it, but does not find time to read it.
- Person C: Knows of a good book and buys it, starts reading it, but never finishes it.
- Person D: Knows of a good book and buys it, finishes reading it, but does not implement the lessons learned from the book.
- Person E: Knows of a good book and buys it, finishes reading it, and consistently implements the lessons learned from it.

The difference between Person A and Person E is their level of commitment.

This leads to the question: What does it take for you to have a high level of commitment?

Author and human behavioral specialist Dr John Demartini believes that commitment is a correlation between your voids and your values. This means that if you perceive something to be missing from your life – there is a void – you will place a high value on ensuring that you do what it takes to fill that void.

So, if you perceive that you are missing out on wealth – your void – you will follow the advice, buy the book on wealth, read and finish it, and consistently implement the lessons taught in the book.

Going back to the example of gym: If you easily give up on the goal of becoming fit, perhaps you did not have a big enough void driving you to keep that commitment.

Refer to Chapter Activity 1: "Determine your hierarchy of values."

He who knows others is wise: He who knows himself is enlightened.

LAO TZU

Compete with yourself and not against others

I have grown increasingly fascinated about why people so easily break their commitment to themselves. Upon reflecting on my personal life lessons, I have come to believe the following: Your relationship with commitment is linked to your lessons on competition.

From a young age, we are taught to compete against other people. In school, you may have either been top of the class, or perhaps below average. In university, you may have either been part of the passing statistic, or one of those who was failing. At work, there are performance ratings that classify you as an over-achiever or an average worker. In order to achieve anything that is above average, you adopt a mindset to compete against others. However, when it comes to more personal goals, you will need to adopt a different approach.

I learned this lesson when I was writing the examination that would qualify me to become a Chartered Accountant. I failed the first part of the Board Examination twice; despite achieving an A aggregate in matric and a Dean's Commendation in my first year of university. I could not understand why my friends I tutored in university were passing the examination, but I was failing.

After I failed this examination for a second year in a row, I did some soul searching and realized that my approach to the examination, and more importantly, my thinking, had to change. I had to stop comparing myself to other people at the office who were passing the examination. I began to start comparing my result against my previous best attempt. I chose to compete against myself. I passed the exam on my third attempt – mainly owing to this shift in thinking.

If you would like to increase your level of commitment to achieve your next big goal, compete against your prior best attempt and not against other people. I encourage you to be aware of what people around you are doing – they are your role models – but keep your focus on being the best version of 'you'.

Usain Bolt, the Jamaican sprinter and 100m world record-holder, once said of his performance on the track: "It is less about competing against others and more about competing against yourself."

Empowering and disempowering words

As an executive coach to leaders in business, I can fairly accurately assess your level of commitment to achieving your goals by the words you use. The manner in which you express your thoughts has a direct correlation to how you experience reality.

TABLE 1: *Empowering and disempowering words*

Empowering Words (High Internalization)	I love to	Passion and commitment aligned
	I choose to	A decision has been made
	I commit to	High level of conviction
	I am	Sounds more certain
	I can	Open to trying
Disempowering Words (Low Internalization)	I could / I would like to	Sounds doubtful as to whether the person will execute the task
	I should	Seems as if someone else is convincing you to doing something.
	I want to	Leaves you with a feeling of "wanting-ness"
	I must / I need to	Hints at desperation

Within the table above, I have listed a series of words under the headings Empowering Words and Disempowering Words. Disempowering words tend to have a low level of internalization. This means that you are not yet convinced this is the right decision for you to take. There is still some doubt in your head, or alternatively, someone else is trying to convince you to do something and you are not yet certain what you should do.

Empowering words tend to be used when a person has internalized the impact of their decision, and their passion and commitment to taking action is aligned. I have listed empowering words from the lowest level of "I can" to the highest level of "I love to."

The impact of word choice becomes evident if you consider two people who are being interviewed for a job. Who would you hire for the position: Person A who says "I need this job", or Person B who says "I love this opportunity to…"

In your quest to stay committed to achieving your goals, change the wording of how you express yourself. It is not: "I want to lose weight…" All you will be left with is a feeling of wanting-ness.

Change it to: "I choose to lose weight." By changing the wording, there is more congruency between what your head is thinking and what your heart is feeling. The greater the internalization, the greater your commitment to fulfilling your goal.

Discipline and focus

Once you commit to doing something and you are more aware of your empowered word choice, your next step is to build discipline by being consistent. On average, it takes three months of consistently implementing a new task before it becomes entrenched in one's normal routine.

I regularly teach my students that if you can build the discipline of doing something during winter when it is colder and more challenging, then doing the same task in summer will be easy. You would have built the discipline during the more challenging months.

I firmly believe that discipline is also about being able to wake up early in the morning – consistently. Regardless of whether it is a public holiday, a Saturday or you have the day off work, wake up by 5am. When you wake up early, you have more time to reflect on the day ahead, and more time to get ready for the day. Would you prefer to be the person who has a leisurely shower and enjoys their breakfast, or the person who wakes up late, has a rushed shower and eats breakfast in the car? The manner in which you start your day sets the tone for how you execute your commitment to yourself and to others for the rest of the day.

I learned the value of waking up early in the morning when I was studying for my post-graduate degree while working full-time. To get the most out of the day, I used to wake up at 3am in the morning and study until 6am. After a full day of work, I would spend two hours in the evening completing examination questions on the content I had studied earlier that morning. As hard as it was to balance all of that, I felt a very spiritual connection to waking up early and getting my work done first. When you wake up before everyone else, you will find yourself surrounded by the peace and tranquility of the day. You have honored your commitment to your goal by putting your work first, before other work.

I also believe that the 'snooze' button on our alarm clocks has created a society of lazy people. Every time you hit the snooze button, you are snoozing on your commitment to your day ahead. So, wake up on the first ring of the alarm and start your day.

Being committed to achieving your goal also implies that you will require a high level of focus to ensure it gets done. Focus is like the torchlight you shine into the darkness. The narrower the focus, the higher the definition of the image you are able to see. When you commit to a goal, all of your energy, time and resources are dedicated to fulfilling it.

I once asked my personal fitness trainer to reflect on his clientele and to list the top three factors that differentiated his top achievers: Those individuals who were able to dramatically transform their physique in a specific period of time. This is a summary of what he said:

1. They knew what they wanted. They had a specific goal.
2. They were consistent. They found the time to train in the cold winter months and on public holidays, or on weekends if they were unable to train during the week. These were the people who made up for lost sessions due to work or other schedule clashes and were able to get back on track.
3. They were committed to doing the hard work, both in the gym and on their own. Hard work included improving their diet and training on their own.

ONE – CREATING AWARENESS – COMMITMENT

Those people had three things in common: Focus, discipline and commitment.

Refer to Chapter Activity 2: "Standing out from the crowd."

Persistence and patience

There have been studies compiled on children growing up in some of the hardest conditions; in the toughest of neighborhoods; and in war-torn regions in the world. The children who survive those conditions and go on to make a success of their lives are not necessarily the smartest kids or the strongest people: They are the children who are the most resilient – they are both persistent and patient. These qualities hold true for most people, in most environments.

When striving for your dreams, you will encounter challenges and setbacks. This is normal: It is life's test to assess how determined you are to achieve your goals. Many people are persistent and try different approaches to overcoming their challenges. However, fewer people are both **persistent and patient**. One needs patience to endure hardship until one achieves success. Then, one needs persistence to find creative ways to achieve one's goals and to not give up. To stay committed to achieving your dreams, persistence and its close sibling, patience, go together.

A commitment to yourself

Over the course of your life, you will share your journey with a multitude of people – family, friends, colleagues, acquaintances and life partners. The fact is: There will be many people who enter and exit your life at some point or another. The one person who will remain consistent in your life is you.

I believe that in order to gain control of your life, your first commitment is to fulfill three important goals:

1. **Educate yourself.** Knowledge is power. When you are educated, you are able to control your decision-making and to make wise decisions while pursuing your dreams.
2. **Look after your body.** Make a commitment to yourself to stay healthy and fit. When you are in good shape, you increase your energy state and this enables you to fully enjoy the success you create.
3. **Be financially independent.** When you are in control of your finances, you are in control of a commodity that provides you with the means to fulfill your purpose.

In Part 1 of this chapter, the focus is on the principles to help you stay committed in general aspects of life.

In Part 2 of this chapter, we will explore the principles to becoming financially independent.

PART TWO

COMMITMENT TO YOUR FINANCIAL INDEPENDENCE

Know your values

When I was a newly qualified Chartered Accountant, my favorite mantra was: "Life is short, and we must live for the now!" I had a value system that focused on short-term gratification. As a result, I did not plan financially for the long term and spent most of my money on clothes, entertainment and socializing.

When I relocated cities soon after completing my articles, I realized that although I had earned my qualification, my only other asset was my vast wardrobe of clothing. Despite working and earning money for four years, I did not have any savings to my name.

If you wish to build wealth for yourself, you first need to understand what is important to you. What do you value? I have found that if building wealth is not within the top three of your personal set of values, then you probably do not have sufficient motivation to save.

This is an important principle. Know your values and make building wealth one of your top three.

Understand your limiting beliefs

Beliefs are developed over time. They are usually a mix of cultural upbringing, environmental influences and personal experiences. However, in the process of building personal wealth, some beliefs can become obstacles to achieving personal financial fulfillment.

Some beliefs about money are: "Money is not important"; "Money is evil – it attracts bad luck!"; "Money is bad – it changes you"; or "Money attracts bad company."

The reality is that money is neutral. It is neither good nor bad. It is merely a tool that we use as a form of trade – to exchange one thing for another. What we choose to trade our money for is based on our beliefs, values and personal morals. If you wish to change the experience for which you trade money, then you need to change your beliefs and values about money.

These beliefs could also be holding you back from earning a higher income. For a moment, consider how much money you earn within 12 months. Now ask yourself a question: Is it possible to earn that same amount of money within one month? Of course it is. You first need to believe it. If you are finding it difficult to think of this as a reality, you need to think deeper and explore the belief that is holding you back.

Earning a fixed income brings with it a fixed mentality, which implies fixed beliefs that keep you in a comfort zone. I will talk about this statement in a later chapter.

Another popular money mistake that most people make is the belief that you 'make' money rather than 'earn' it. You will earn money as long as there is a fair exchange for goods and services. The greater the perceived value of the goods or services being traded, the greater the amount of money you will earn.

So it is wise to identify whether you have any limiting beliefs about money, and to start replacing them with more empowering beliefs about building wealth for yourself.

Determine your purpose for money

In order to attract large amounts of money, you need a big enough purpose for it. When your purpose is big enough, the 'how to earn it' becomes easier to figure out.

The best way to earn large amounts of money is by owning your own business. You earn money by first knowing your own purpose in life, and then aligning your purpose to the purpose of your business.

Set up your business in such a way that you focus on solving problems for vast numbers of people. The more efficiently you solve a problem for a vast number of people, the more money you will earn. This means that, in time, you will need to set up the business with systems, processes and people in place to allow the business to function without you physically being there. At that point, you will start to earn large sums of money.

But, always remember: Earning large sums of money starts with finding your purpose for the money.

Refer to Chapter Activity 3: "Action steps to attract more money."

Attaining financial freedom

To understand the concept of financial freedom, we first need to understand a very important principle: When you do not have money (are broke), you do not help anyone else on a larger scale in life. As long as you are broke, you are probably considered to be a 'taker' – someone who gets money from other people, including family, friends and social security systems. The problem with being a taker is that it robs you of the dignity to live your own life and make decisions for yourself.

The second principle in creating financial freedom has everything to do with energy. In order to earn huge amounts of money, you need to have huge amounts of energy. It takes huge energy in the form of effort, time, and commitment to do all of the hard work required to earn money. The problem is that most people are not prepared to do the hard work involved with earning large amounts of money.

Energy is transferable: It is able to move from one form to another. Consider how lightning comes about: It is created from static tension in the clouds (energy) that grows so intense that it becomes visible as lightning. If the force is strong enough, the lightning can also cause damage to the surface of the Earth. Likewise, if you as an individual have low energy, not many people will want to do business with you. People with large amounts of energy naturally attract more people to work with them.

The key to success is raising your energy levels. I believe that time management is more about how you manage your **energy** in the time available to you than about how you manage your tasks in the **limited time available**. Your energy levels are directly proportional to your levels of fitness. It is one thing to have a goal of becoming financially independent, but if you are unfit and unhealthy, you will not have the stamina to do what needs to be done, and you will not be able to enjoy the fruits of your hard work. It is for this reason that I believe you should focus on being both financially independent, and fit and healthy.

Refer to Chapter Activity 4: "Staying fit and healthy."

Pay yourself first

Having **self-discipline** and **high self-worth** are essential factors in building wealth. To illustrate this, consider the usual spending path for a person at month end:
1. Pay debt first.
2. Pay credit cards and bills.
3. Pay lifestyle expenses.
4. Pay yourself (save) if there is any money left over.

To change to a savings culture, a person's spending path should be as follows:
1. Pay yourself first (save).
2. Pay taxes.
3. Pay your lifestyle expenses.
4. Pay bills according to their priority.

When you pay yourself first, it can be likened to harvesting the best of the crop versus waiting for the dregs after everyone else has taken their share. It is also more psychologically inspiring to see your savings grow than to focus on your debt.

Start saving

Determine your monthly income and commit to saving either 10% of your income or a specific amount – whichever is greater.

Open a separate bank account in which to deposit this amount each month, knowing that you will, in essence, be paying yourself first.

There are some rules for this account:
1. Once the money has been deposited, it **cannot** be used for any purpose other than to earn you a greater level of income.
2. Your savings are not to be used for any type of emergency or holiday expenses. If you wish to travel, save for this separately, **after** you have paid yourself first.
3. Let the interest you earn on the total value accumulate within the same account, giving you the benefits of compound interest.
4. You need to ultimately consider the money in this account as your 'employees', who are working for you to earn you more income.

Every quarter, run a projection of how much income you will have by a certain age, if you commit to your savings plan. This exercise will further inspire you to stick to your plan.

Refer to Chapter Activity 5: "Simple budgeting tips."

Increase the amount you save

Every three months increase the amount you save by 10%. So if you started saving $100, for instance, your savings would look like this:

Month:

1	2	3	4	5	6	7	8	9
$100	$100	$100	$110	$110	$110	$121	$121	$121

And in month 10, you would increase your savings to $133 for the next three months, and so the cycle goes.

On average, it takes about three months before a new behavior breaks an old habit. Apply this principle in the context of saving. If you continue saving a fixed amount indefinitely, the value of the amount saved will no longer inspire you and you will become bored. It is usually at this stage that you find other purposes for your money and are diverted from your ultimate goal of saving.

You can also liken the above to the economic principle of supply and demand. When you place a demand on yourself to save a higher amount, you are supplied with more to look after.

What is important in this early stage of saving is not the amount that you save, but building the habit and discipline to save.

Create a cushion account

At some point, you will encounter some form of financial emergency. This might take the form of a medical bill, an unforeseen accident or household repair, or a family-related expense. When these costs arise, you do not want to pay for these expenses from your hard-earned savings!

To avoid this, build a reserve of cash in addition to your savings equal to 2 to 3 months' worth of your current income. If you currently earn $10k per month, you should have a cushion account of at least $20k to $30k that you fund unforeseen emergencies from.

In times of financial distress, these emergency expenses can be funded from your reserve account.

Create multiple streams of income

Talk to a financial adviser. He or she will introduce you to the concept of a diversified portfolio of investments. This will help you to spread your risk while still earning a regular stream of income.

As long as you are earning income from only one source, you are carrying too much of a financial risk. You, too, need to hold a diversified portfolio of investments.

Long-term wealth requires long-term discipline

Building wealth involves adopting a **rational** and **disciplined** step-by-step approach.

STEP 1: Draw up a budget

Create a 12-month budget for yourself. This should be updated each year.

Each month compare your actual expenses with your budget. Reflect on any deviations and make the necessary changes:

1. For the months when your total expenses exceed your budget, investigate the reasons this happened. If needed, implement a change in lifestyle expenses to self-manage your budget.
2. For the months when your total actual expenses are lower than your budget, transfer what you have saved to your reserve or cushion account. Doing this allows you to increase your savings rather than spend your money on low-priority items.

STEP 2: Start saving

Once you have started budgeting and have applied the principles of saving, you should have built up at least one month's worth of income in your personal bank account that earns 3–5% interest on average. You would have also disciplined yourself to make a monthly deposit into your separate savings account, which will yield 6–8% (typically a money market account). You are now ready to accept a higher level of interest risk.

STEP 3: Invest in low-risk investments

For the next stage, find a suitable investment, which could be **unit trusts, government bonds, property and equity investments** that will yield **interest, rental** or **dividend income** with between 5–7% return. Ultimately, the investment at this level should be slightly higher than the interest being earned in your personal bank account. Keep making deposits into this investment until it equals **two months** of your monthly income.

STEP 4: Invest in medium to high-risk investments

Over time, you will hold investments that will yield higher rates of return, with each successive level holding the equivalent of two months' worth of your income. As a result, you should invest the equivalent of two months' income in a range of portfolios, as shown in the table that follows:

TABLE 2: *Rates of investment*

Investment vehicle	Rate of return	Type of investor
Reserves	3–5%	Low risk/beginner
Low-risk investments	5–7%	Low risk/beginner
Mid-tiered risk investments	7–9%	Medium risk/intermediate
Mid-tiered risk investments	9–11%	Medium risk/intermediate
High-risk investments	11–13% 14% +	High risk/advanced

Consult with your financial adviser to provide you with insights into which investments or stocks to purchase to yield the kinds of returns indicated above.

Every year, review your portfolio and the returns that you have actually earned from your investments. When I conduct my own financial review, I usually wind down some investments that might not be doing that well; I re-allocate funds to new investments that have more potential to grow; and I top-up investments that are achieving consistent yields. When it comes to building your wealth, you cannot have an attitude of investing once-off and hope that all goes as planned. By constantly reviewing your portfolio, you can effect major changes to sustain your increased returns.

Some people might ask: Why not first invest in instruments that yield a return in excess of 14%, since they are available? This strategy is similar to the concept of climbing the corporate ladder. As an employee starting to work for a company, you do not start your first day as the director of the company. You start at a beginner position, which is a relatively lower-risk position than a director position. You first need to show that you are **able to deal with low- and mid-tiered risk** before you can be promoted to more senior, riskier positions. I have seen people invest in high-return stock too quickly. They get all excited about their big returns, only to lose their money a few months later and feel depressed. This is because they have not built up their risk tolerance from a lower level upwards. They were looking for a quick return without learning first how to manage risk.

The concept of 'mo-ployees'

Whether you are a business owner or an employee at work, you are essentially working for someone else – your clients or your employer. Whatever your position, you could have employees working for you. This could take the form of outsourced partners or direct reports.

Just as you have multiple streams of people working with and around you to make your business or work assignments successful, the same should apply to your relationship with money. Money is merely a conduit through which goods and services flow.

Money is like an employee who is working for you. As long as you invest your money into a diversified portfolio of investments, your money will work for you and earn you income. Your job is to manage your 'mo-ployees' (money employees) to ensure that your money is being as productive as possible.

Show that you can handle more money

Imagine that your first job is as a bank teller in a huge banking company. Since you have just started and the manager is still getting

ONE – CREATING AWARENESS – COMMITMENT

to know you, he gives you a float of $1k to look after. Every day, for six months, you look after that cash float. You account for any 'overs' and 'unders', to the dollar.

You do such a great job that the manager then promotes you to look after $5k. Again, every day for six months you look after that float of money, reconciling to the last dollar.

Your manager is impressed and promotes you to a better position, in which you look after $15k. And so, you continue your good work.

Using this analogy in your life, you will be given a bigger and bigger 'float of money' to look after – as long as you can show that you are mature and wise enough to take care of it.

Back to reality

In life, you are like that bank teller. You are tested every day on how well you are looking after the money that has been given to you. From your very first position at work to your current role, the level of income you earn is directly proportional to the amount of income you prove that you can manage.

The Universe will give you exactly the amount of money that you can handle.

Refer to Chapter Activity 6: "Become a student of life."

We have covered a lot of ground in Part 1 and Part 2 of this chapter on commitment. The foundation of instilling change in your life has now been firmly laid.

Next, let us explore how awareness has a role to play in helping you entrench control in your life.

CHAPTER 1

QUESTIONS AND ANSWERS

Q It can take so long to make a decision to commit, let alone keep a commitment. This is all such hard work – is there not an easier way to achieve success in life?

A No, there is no such thing as overnight success. Consistent hard work is the only secret to success, and commitment is your starting point.

Q I like the concept of 'empowering' versus 'disempowering' words. What if I go back to my bad habits and start using disempowering words again?

A Awareness is a very powerful tool to bring about change. Become aware every time you think of a disempowering word, or you say it out loud. Immediately change the word to something within the empowering word list. Over time, you will start to auto-correct yourself.

Q I am not a qualified Chartered Accountant like you. Although I followed the concepts of how to become financially independent, I don't think I can do this by myself.

A Firstly, relax. What you say to yourself, you become. You do not have to be a qualified accountant to become astute at handling your personal finances. Within that chapter, I covered the basic structure of how to become financially independent. As long as you understand what you need to do, you can consult with your financial adviser about putting your plan into action. Knowing how to create wealth for yourself is a skill that can be learned. If you are interested in finding out more, invest in books, workshops, short courses and conferences to educate yourself further on this topic. Most importantly, do not waste time. Start your financial independence plan and use the benefit of time to build wealth for yourself.

🗨 Closing affirmations

1. I am focused. I am disciplined. I am committed.
2. I am persistent. I am patient. I overcome my challenges.
3. I am a money magnet. The more I save, the more money I am given to manage.
4. The more money I manage, the more I am given to manage.
5. My body is my temple. I look after my body, which is my vehicle to achieving my goals in life.

TAKE ACTION
CHAPTER 1 ACTIVITIES

Commitment

Observe

Nest

Tactics

Re-enforcement

Opposition

Life

■ Activity 1: *Determine your hierarchy of values*

A value is something that is important to you. Owing to the importance of that value, you would do anything to ensure that the value is met.

You have a unique set of values that you live by. These values define who you are and provide you with reasons for doing what you do.

Complete the following activity to identify your unique set of values.

On a clean page, draw 3 columns with 12 rows, and write down the answers to each of the following questions. Note that for each question, you are looking for your top 3 answers. When you write down your response, keep it within 2 to 3 words per column. This will make it easier for you to analyze. Once you are done, you will have 36 responses in total. Ensure that you do not leave blank spaces in any of the columns.

Your page would look something like the template opposite.

Your value system will become more evident as you answer the 12 simple questions.

Value questions

1. How do you spend your time?

Take a look at how you allocate your waking hours. What claims most of your day? You need to consider an entire week from Monday to Sunday. Think of everything that you do from the time that you wake up to the time that you go to sleep.

Explanation:
If you are mostly working, then your career is probably important to you. One of the items that you write down will be 'work'. Then, think of how your time is spent after work. If you go to the gym for one hour every day, then write down 'exercise' in the next column. Perhaps you go out socializing. If so, write down 'socializing' in one

ONE – CREATING AWARENESS – COMMITMENT

No.	Question	Response/ Column 1	Response/ Column 2	Response/ Column 3
1.	How do you spend your time?			
2.	Where in your life are you most disciplined?			
3.	Where in your life are you most organized?			
4.	How do you spend your money?			
5.	How do you fill your space?			
6.	What do you speak about with others?			
7.	Who do you admire? Why?			
8.	If you had the means, where would you travel?			
9.	When you think of success, what comes to mind?			
10.	List three things you would like to accomplish in the next five years.			
11.	What is your next big step?			
12.	What is your message?			

of the columns. Perhaps from work you go straight home to spend time with your family, If you do, then put down 'family' in one of the columns.

Instruction:
In row 1, write down what you spend **most** of your time on in column 1, **second-most** time on in column 2, and **third-most** time on in column 3. Remember to keep your responses between 2 to 3 words per column.

2. Where in your life are you most disciplined?

Everyone is focused somewhere in their life. Where are you consistently on task?

Explanation:
If you place a high value on something, then no one needs to remind you to do something. As an example, I place a high value on my work. No one needs to remind me to write an article for a magazine or complete a report for my client. Regardless of the day or time, I will find the time to do it. I am also disciplined with my eating habits. Very seldom do I eat out as I place a high value on healthy home-cooked meals. So, diet is another high value for me. Now consider your own life, and think of those areas where you do what you need to do regardless of how tired you are or the time of the day.

Instruction:
In row 2, write down where in your life you are the **most** disciplined in column 1, **second-most** disciplined in column 2, and **third-most** disciplined in column 3.

3. Where in your life are you most organized?

Ask yourself: "Where is there the greatest order in my life? Where do things run smoothly with the least amount of volatility?"

Explanation:

You tend to have a high level of organization in areas of your life that are important to you. I enjoy cooking, so if you have to look around my kitchen, you will find that I have all my spices in individual containers that make it easy for me to cook. I also have a high level of organization with my books. Education and wisdom hold high value for me. My books are organized by genre and by topic – this makes it easy for me to locate books for my research. Now think of your own life and consider where you have a high level of organization.

Instruction:

In row 3, write down where in your life you are **most** organized in column 1, **second-most** organized in column 2, and **third-most** organized in column 3.

4. How do you spend your money?

Look at how you spend your money.

Explanation:

Think about what you spend money on, after you have paid for your fixed expenses, including debit orders and monthly installments. The trends in your variable spending will give you insight into what you value most. People who value their children and their family will spend on gifts and items for their family first before buying something for themselves. If you value entertainment and socializing with your friends, you will always find that extra cash to go out and have fun.

Instruction:

In row 4, write down what you spend the **most** money on in column 1, **second-most** money on in column 2, and **third-most** money on in column 3.

5. How do you fill your space?

Reflect on a space that is your own. It could be your workstation, your vehicle or your home. With what do you fill your space?

Explanation:
The manner in which you fill your space reflects what is important to you. A person who fills their space with family pictures sends the message that family is important to them. A person who fills their space with their graduation certificates is subtly saying that education is important to them. If you look at my space, as an example, you will usually find a book or a magazine that I am reading with a note pad and pen in almost every room, as I am always reading something of research value.

Instruction:
In row 5, write down what you first **most** fill your space with in column 1, what you **second-most** fill your space with in column 2, and **third-most** fill your space with in column 3.

6. What do you speak about with others?

When you meet someone new, with what topics do you engage? When you are with friends and family, what topics do you revisit time and time again? The topics that you are comfortable speaking about are aligned to your values. When something is important to you, you tend to speak about it with other people.

Explanation:
After opening a conversation with talk about the weather, traffic and general news, what are the top three topics you always ending up discussing? As an example, my work is about leadership development, so I usually engage in conversations with other people about this topic.

I am fascinated by the drivers of human behavior and the different techniques to motivate and inspire people. I also place a high value on fitness and exercise. In my conversations with others, I enjoy talking about the different ways in which people stay fit and the types of outdoor competitive sports in which people take part.

Instruction:
In row 6, write down what you **most** talk to others about in column 1; **second-most** talk to others about in column 2; and **third-most** talk to others about in column 3.

7. Who do you admire? Why?

Think about the names of three people you admire. Write down in three words or less why you admire them.

Explanation:
The people whom we admire, and the aspect that we admire in them, provides insight into what we value in life. The people that you admire can vary: it could be a celebrity, your parent, your sibling, a friend, a family member or a work colleague. It does not really matter who the person is – just think of three people that you admire. Once you have identified the names of these people, write down in three words or less what you most admire about them. As an example, you may admire your mum's resilient nature; or the fact that Steve Jobs is a creative genius.

Instruction:
In row 7, from your insights above, write down the qualities you **most** admire in person 1 in column 1, **most** admire in person 2 in column 2, and **most** admire in person 3 in column 3.

8. If you had the means, where would you travel?

Let us imagine that you had the ability to travel anywhere in the world – where would you go to? Think about the exact destination. Do not just say you want to visit the United States of America, or you would like to tour Australia. Instead, be specific and write down New York, or the Great Barrier Reef, or the Eiffel Tower in Paris.

Then write down in three words or less why you would like to visit that particular place.

Perhaps you want to visit New York because it is the metro-hub; and your adventurous spirit wants to visit Australia; and finally, you would like to visit Paris with your significant other because it is romantic.

Explanation:
This question not only provides insight into the places that you would like to visit, but also into the underlying value that is driving your desire to go there.

Instruction:
In row 8, write down what you **most** value in destination 1 in column 1, **most** value in destination 2 in column 2, and **most** value in destination 3 in column 3.

9. When you think of success, what comes to mind first?

Each one of us has our own unique definition of success. When we think of success, we usually have in mind a person who epitomizes success for us. What you admire in others, you are striving for in yourself. The people whom you perceive to be successful represent the success that you see for yourself. The areas of life in which you perceive them to be successful provide insight into your own values.

Explanation:

Think about the three people who epitomize success for you. Write down the names of these individuals, and then, in brackets, write down in three words or less what is it about them that you believe makes them successful. As an example, perhaps you find your uncle successful because he is an entrepreneur; or you admire your sister, who is able to balance a full-time career and being a mum to two children.

Instruction:

In row 9, write down what success **most** means to you in person 1 in column 1, **most** means to you in person 2 in column 2, and **most** means to you in person 3 in column 3.

10. List three things you would like to accomplish in the next five years.

Next, I would like you to reflect on your long-term goals. Think about what you would like to achieve within the next three to five years.

Explanation:

Your long-term goals are driven by an inner desire, which in turn hints at your hierarchy of values. If in the long term you are planning to complete a degree or attain a qualification, then education is a high value for you. If you are planning to save for a house, then wealth and finances are a high value for you. If you are planning to get married and start a family, then family and personal relationship are a high value for you.

Instruction:
Within row 10, write down what you would first **most** like to accomplish within column 1, **second-most** like to accomplish in column 2, and **third-most** like to accomplish in column 3.

11. What's the next big step you need to take?

Now, I would like you to think about the top three goals that you would like to achieve within the next 6 to 12 months. The answer to this question reveals your short-term goals. Since you tend to set goals in areas of your life that have a high importance to you, the answers to this question further reveals your top three values.

Explanation:
Perhaps within the next 6 to 12 months you are seeking a career change and will be attending interviews for your next position. This would imply that career and work are important to you. Maybe you are planning a holiday with family or friends and have started a savings account for this purpose. If your ultimate aim is to spend cash on a social activity, then socializing is a high value.

Instruction:
In row 11, write down the **biggest** goal you need to achieve in column 1, the **second-biggest** goal you need to achieve in column 2, and the **third-biggest** goal you need to achieve in column 3.

12. If you had the opportunity to get a message across to a large group of people, what would it be?

Let us assume that I am about to give you an opportunity to speak to a group of people. You can speak to this group of people on any topic that is a passion of yours. What are the top three topics that you would speak to this audience about.

Explanation:

When something is important to you and you feel strongly about it, you become passionate about sharing that message with other people. So, as an example, someone who has overcome obesity will want to speak on the topic of health. A woman who has struggled to educate herself and become financially independent may wish to speak to other young women on how they can do the same. Or consider the person who grew up in poverty and became successful through thrifty and ingenious methods of saving – this person may wish to speak about the importance of saving.

Instruction:

In row 12, write down what message you would first **most** like to convey in column 1, **second-most** like to convey in column 2, and **third-most** like to convey in column 3.

Ensure that you have three answers for each of the 12 questions – 36 responses in total.

Next, scan through the list and summarize the items that appeared most often. You are looking for your TOP FIVE values. Look out for any words that are synonyms. You can summarize these under one all-encompassing word. For example, if you valued exercise, and throughout the list you had words like 'gym', 'exercise', and 'running', you can group all of these words under 'Fitness' with a count of 3 to indicate the number of times it came up in the list. Continue to review your list until you have accounted for all 36 responses.

Once you have summarized your responses, list the top five categories that came out most often. So, you could have grouped your items under 'family' or 'work' or 'fitness' or 'socializing' or 'religion', as an example.

If two categories came up the same number of times – if, say, family and education individually came up on the list seven times – you need to determine which one is more important in the hierarchy. Ask yourself a simple question. If you had a finite amount of time this weekend and you could either spend time with your family, or sacrifice family time in order to study for an examination and gain your qualification, what would you do? The answer to this question will reveal which of the two categories is a higher value to you.

But, what if you look at the outcome of this exercise and you are not happy with your current hierarchy of values?

Say that your outcome of this exercise is as follows:

1. Work
2. Family
3. Socializing
4. Spirituality
5. Fitness

Out of interest, you tend to focus your time, money, energy and resources on your top three values. Anything else that is below the top three values gets the leftovers in terms of your time, money, energy and resources. You should also review your top three values and compare them to your top three goals. If your values and your goals are not aligned, then you will probably find it difficult to achieve those goals.

To elevate a value that is further down the list into your top three values, for instance, let's say that you would like fitness and health to be within your top three values, complete the following further exercise.

Step 1: Write down 50–75 *general* reasons why it is important for you to achieve fitness and health in your life. As you write these statements down, you may find that some of them are repetition. This is good, as you are entrenching in your mind the importance of getting this done.

Step 2: Write down 50–75 *specific* reasons why becoming healthy and fit will help you within the other seven areas of life – these areas of life are in bold below. **Health and fitness** is one of the seven areas of life. So, think about how being healthy and fit will help you:
1. In your **career**
2. With your **education**
3. In your **personal relationships** and with your family
4. With your **spirituality**
5. In your **social circle** and in society
6. With your **finances and wealth**.

As you go through life stages, your values shift, too. So it is wise to regularly evaluate your hierarchy of values and to compare your top three values to your top three short-term goals that you wish to achieve, to ensure that your values and your goals are in alignment.

■ Activity 2: *Standing out from the crowd*

There are three traits that can set you apart from others:
1. **Discipline**: To train yourself to uphold your commitment.
2. **Creativity**: To learn how to come up with new solutions and ideas.
3. **The ability to synthesize information**: To be able to draw your own conclusions from a variety of resources.

As you progress in your career and your education, find ways to do the following:
1. Complete your tasks on time. This helps to build discipline.
2. Become fascinated with different forms of art. This ignites creative thought.
3. Assist work colleagues with their deadlines. This builds further discipline and teaches you about teamwork.
4. Read inspiring poetry. This inspires you to think creatively.

5. Get involved with sport. In order to succeed at sport, disciplined training is required.
6. Read extensively. This helps you think holistically and synthesize disparate concepts.
7. Exercise your body on a daily basis. This builds good discipline.
8. Stay curious and ask questions. This helps you to synthesize concepts and better understand them.
9. Learn from your mistakes. This is how you become more creative at problem-solving.
10. Play games and have fun. This builds creative and innovative thought processes.

■ Activity 3: *Action steps to attract more money*

1. Investment

If you want to attract more money, show that you can manage what you currently have through continuous investment and re-investment.

2. Promotions and bonuses

When you receive a promotion or bonus, do not spend the bulk of the money. Instead, invest a higher proportion of the income in investments that will earn you more income. When your income increases, do not increase your lifestyle expenses by the same proportion as the increase in your income. Instead, marginally increase your lifestyle expenses, and invest more of your income into your savings.

3. Save extra income

Let's say you budgeted to spend $5k a month. Instead, you spent $4.5k. For some reason, you saved $0.5k. Instead of spending this money, transfer it into a savings account.

We all budget for things that we want to buy ourselves. Let's imagine you wanted to buy yourself a new perfume or an aftershave. Before you could actually buy it, someone else bought it for you. Transfer the money you would have spent on the perfume into your savings. Any dividends or interest that you earn from invested funds should be reinvested into the principal amount.

4. Re-evaluate your values

Conduct a review to see whether saving or investing money was in your top three values. If not, something else will always get in the way of you saving and earning a higher income. In order to elevate the value you place on earning and saving more money, list 50–75 *general* benefits of money coming into your hands.

Then, write down 50–75 *specific* benefits of money coming into your hands, and how these will help you in the six other areas of your life.

Refer to Activity 1 in this chapter for an explanation of how to determine your hierarchy of values and the seven areas of life.

5. Commit to a big cause for your money

Think about the reasons why money should flow into your hands. Will the money be used to satisfy only your personal needs, or is it also for the benefit of other people, too? The higher your cause, the greater the probability of money flowing to you.

The cause for your money needs to be bigger than your immediate needs. For example, when Bill Gates set about creating his company, Microsoft, he had a personal mission (cause), which was to ensure that every desktop had a computer. His cause was clearly bigger than his own immediate needs of having one computer on his own desk.

Is your cause big enough? If not, then your cause or purpose for the money needs to be re-evaluated.

Activity 4: *Staying fit and healthy*

Simple actions to keeping fit

1. **Maintain strong abdominal muscles – your core**

Your abdominal muscles can be likened to the engine room of your body. The stronger your abdominal muscles, the fitter you are. Each day exercise your abdominal muscles with a range of crunches, sit-ups, leg-lifts, and press-ups.

Attending a weekly Pilates or yoga class at your gym not only helps to keep your abdominal muscles in peak condition, it also improves your flexibility.

2. **Increase your cardiovascular exercises**

Any movement that pushes the heart rate up and increases blood circulation is good for your body. Cardio helps you to improve your heart rate; increase metabolism; and improve your hormonal profile by releasing 'good' hormones into your body.

If you have the go-ahead from your doctor, introduce a cardio exercise into your weekly regimen. Consider running, cycling, jogging, or something similar. Apart from feeling good after the exercise, these activities will also help you to keep your body fit for life.

3. **Enter recreational races or participate in sports challenges**

If you have not been exercising regularly, then another way to get you back into the regimen is to enter a running race, or another sporting challenge of your choice. Should you have any particular health concerns, visit your doctor before embarking on any form of exercise.

Knowing that you have a 20km road race to prepare for in eight months' time will motivate you to go to the gym and begin your training.

In addition, if you enter a race that requires a team of people to participate – like a relay race at work or in your community – then knowing that you are part of a team that needs to be there on the day gives you an added reason to keep up your exercise routine.

Once the race is over and you have successfully completed it, then find another race to enter – perhaps one with an added challenge to stretch you even further.

4. Keep a food journal

You may find that despite the regular exercise and visits to the gym, you are not slimming down. This is probably owing to the fact that you are not eating correctly.

Purchase a journal in which you diarize everything you have eaten for the day. Write down what you ate; the portion size; the time you ate it; and how you felt afterwards. Do this for a month and then conduct an analysis.

Depending on your analysis, you might want to make some changes for month 2. For example, you may want to drink more water during the day. Maintain your food journal for the next two months.

After month 3, make more adjustments based on your reflection of your progress to date.

Continue to maintain your journal until you have achieved your target fitness level. Some people have found benefit in maintaining a food journal for up to 12 months. If you take your health and fitness seriously, then a food journal is for you.

5. Train with someone else

Consider finding an accountability coach who will help you stay committed to your fitness goals. This could take the form of a friend who trains with you; a personal trainer who coaches you along with your exercises; a fitness club or association of which you become a member; or a group of you who motivate each other during a training session.

Fueling your system

1. Water

You should be starting your day with a glass of water. Try to avoid caffeinated drinks and hot teas. These essentially drain you of the energy you need for the day. When you add sugar to your hot beverages, the sugar further distorts your energy levels.

Carry around your own bottle of water for the day. Purchase a one-liter container that reminds you of all the water you need to drink.

Drink natural still water. No sugary water, sparkling water or unnaturally flavored water.

2. Eat breakfast

Consume breakfast within two hours of waking up. If you think you are not hungry enough to eat, you have trained your body not to feel hungry in the morning. This is not good if you want to fuel your body for the day ahead.

A small portion of fruit, yogurt or some cereal is all it takes to give your body a bit of energy. We do not drive our vehicle if it has no fuel in it. Likewise, you should not leave the house without adequately 'fueling' your system.

3. In-between snacks

Every two hours, snack on foods like nuts, seeds (sunflower, sesame or pumpkin), or munch on a health bar. Before snacking, remember to drink water, as you could also be dehydrated.

Do not allow yourself to skip snacks. As you get more and more hungry during the day, missing meals will lead to you making unhealthy meal choices.

Carry around your own snacks for the day to avoid missing out on your nutrition. You may have unique food tastes and sensitivities, so consult with a dietitian, who will tailor-make a meal plan for your dietary needs.

4. Main meals

Prepare your own salad for lunch. Ideally, it should contain some form of protein, carbohydrates, fiber, water and lipids (healthy fats).

When eating out, opt for smaller dishes. If the dish is too large, share the excess with someone else, or ask for a smaller portion.

When you overeat, your body will be using the energy to digest the food, rather than to provide the energy you need.

Eat your last meal for the day at least two to three hours before going to sleep. Get into a routine of eating at set times of the day.

5. Enjoy your meals

In some countries, it is considered rude to rush through a meal. Food is meant to be savored and enjoyed. The next time you eat, do it slowly. Be aware of the textures and flavors of the food in your mouth. Chew your food thoroughly.

It takes about 10 to 20 minutes for your body to feel full and send this message to your brain. Take your time eating, or you may overeat without even being aware of it.

Drink water with your main meals rather than any other beverage. Water is a simple medium that aids digestion.

When you eat, try to ensure that your plate is filled with color in the form of vegetables. Eliminate or reduce eating fast foods. These are usually over-processed or over-refined, and lack the essential nutrients that your body needs to sustain a healthy system.

Look after your health

1. Routine medical check-ups

Undergo a yearly medical check-up to test your blood glucose and cholesterol levels, blood pressure, HIV status, and to eliminate the possibility for cancer-related illnesses.

2. Early detection self-checks

Regularly check your body for any lumps, abnormal bruising, and rashes. Be attuned to any unusual aches or discomfort that you might be feeling, such as persistent headaches.

It is best to visit your doctor soon after detection for further investigation, rather than waiting for the problem to become worse.

3. Participate in a loyalty program that credits you for looking after your health

There are plenty of loyalty programs for which you could sign up that will reward you for regular health check-ups and going to the gym. Most of these programs are aligned to your medical aid or life insurance policy.

Apart from receiving a financial reward or retail discounts, you also have an opportunity to improve your health. So, sign-up.

4. Cut the drugs, alcohol and cigarettes

Drugs, alcohol, and cigarettes all impact your levels of thinking. They damage your body, accelerate the aging process, and slow down your progress towards achieving your goals.

Smoking, specifically, stains your teeth, increases your risk of lung cancer, and alters the quality of your voice. If you think of a beautiful luxury vehicle, smoke is one of the waste elements expelled from the exhaust system. Using this analogy, it makes no sense why you would willingly inhale smoke that harms your system.

Drugs and alcohol eventually kill. In the end, the only winner is the drug or alcohol. The tragic deaths of famous celebrities, such as Whitney Houston, Michael Jackson, and Elvis Presley, remind us that addiction to drugs and alcohol can only end in tragedy.

5. Reduce your intake of medication

Keep a journal of the medication that you take on a regular basis. This includes medication for common ailments, such as headaches, sinusitis, and body aches. Many contain some form of alcohol or chemical that can become addictive. Prolonged use of these drugs could also have other side effects, like kidney or liver damage and stomach ulcers. Most people take prescription drugs without reading the side effects on the warning slips. Do not be one of these people. Take the time to educate yourself on the benefits and potential effects of the medication.

It is better to spend time trying to fix the problem naturally than taking medication on an ongoing basis. The role of medication is to temporarily help your body stabilize itself again. Once you reach this point of stability, wean yourself off the medication and allow your body's natural immune system to take over.

6. Manage allergies and intolerances

Keep track of any adverse reactions you may have to certain foods. This could include a bloated abdomen after eating bread, headaches after eating strong cheese, or inflammation after eating certain foods, such as fish, eggs and nuts.

All of these bodily reactions hint at possible allergies and food intolerances that should be eliminated from your diet if you are to attain optimal health.

If you suspect that you could have a food allergy, visit your doctor to conduct tests to confirm the existence of the allergy, as well as any other allergies that may be unknown to you at the time.

■ Activity 5: *Simple budgeting tips*

1. Draw up a spending 'love list'

Make a list of everything you would love to purchase with your income, including a monetary value or budget for that item. For example, you would love to purchase a new television set for $1 000.

Next, for each item, set a realistic date by when you would love to purchase these items. This date could be within the next 12 months, or the next two years, or longer.

Finally, make a summary of the items you intend to purchase over the next 12 months. This list will be used to create your master budget.

2. Create your master budget

Plan to spend two to three hours reviewing your spending patterns over the past 12 months. This will give you the basis of your budget for the next 12 months.

Set up your budget with a spreadsheet package, using the format of an Income Statement:

- **Income**
- **Fixed expenses** (monthly expenses that are fixed in amount, such as rent and insurance)
- **Variable overheads** (expenses that fluctuate in the amount or time of spending, such as clothing and travel).

Include items from your love list, with the amount that you have budgeted for yourself.

To enhance your master budget, you can also use the same expense categories that are found in Annual Financial Statements. For example:

telephone; printing and stationery; travel and accommodation; and medical expenses.

If you use this approach (highly recommended!), I would suggest that you split up certain categories, such as motor vehicle expenses, into their components to make it easier to track your expenses. For instance: Petrol, parking and toll fees.

Budget for expenses that you know will be due in specific months. For instance: Birthday gifts; travel; payment of annual subscriptions; and medical check-ups. The more detail you include in your budget, the more effective you become at managing your personal finances. Also include the amount of money that you transfer into your savings account each month.

In summary, your budget should have 12 columns reflecting each month of budgeted income and expenses for a calendar year, as well as a Year-to-Date cumulative total. Within each expense category in each month, you will have a budgeted amount in line with what you expect to purchase and save over the next 12 months.

3. Monitor your spending

After setting up your budget, your next step is to keep track of every cent you earn and spend.

Each month, analyze your invoices and receipts and record your spending in your spreadsheet, against the categories and the amounts that you have budgeted to spend. Review your bank statements for all electronic payments made, and to monitor any suspicious transactions on your account. If you tend to draw cash to spend, then you need to keep notes and slips to record how you have spent your cash.

As you conduct this exercise each month, you will find that you become more financially astute. You will also become more determined to adjust your spending patterns to align with your budget projections.

4. Get your timing right

Be wise and time your purchases to take advantage of commercial trade. For example, purchase perfumes and jewelry in February (Valentine's Day specials). Buy your stationery to coincide with Back-to-School promotions. Enjoy a spa treatment in May to cash in on Mother's Day discounts. Purchase your groceries at month-end or during special promotions to benefit from commercial trade discounts.

With careful planning, discipline and patience, you can purchase what you planned to buy at reduced rates, leaving you with more money to add to your savings.

5. Benchmark prices before spending

Benchmarking is an exercise used in business to compare a company's products, services and pricing to those of their competitors. This helps a company to refine its competitive strategy. You, too, can use benchmarking for the purpose of maximizing your personal wealth.

Benchmark the prices of all products and services that you anticipate buying before you actually spend. As an example, make a list of all your grocery items and compare the prices between various retailers. You will soon find a store that saves you more money in the longer term.

Conduct the same exercise with items of clothing, cosmetics and furniture – in fact, every item you purchase. This might take time in the short term, but will save you more money going forward.

As you develop the habit of cross-checking prices against competitors and conducting your own research into a product or service, you will gain a new understanding of the pricing and quality of products that you purchase. Soon it will be difficult for anyone to fool you into purchasing an item that costs more than its true worth!

6. Invest in quality

It is wiser to invest in buying quality products rather than substitutes that require regular replacement, which costs more money overall. This principle applies to clothing, cleaning agents, appliances, shoes and bags, to name a few.

Quality products require a little more investment, but by timing your purchases, you can obtain a good price for a product that will last longer and save you money in the longer term.

7. Purchase in bulk and choose refills where possible

Make a list of the items that you use every day, such as detergents, cosmetics and cooking products. Be on the lookout for discounts on these products during month-end promotions, and purchase the items in bulk. For example, instead of buying a 150ml bottle of hair shampoo, choose the 500ml bottle. This principle can also extend to refills. For example, spend more to purchase the larger packaging upfront and then purchase refills, which save you having to purchase the packaging again.

Purchasing in bulk on essential items saves you money in the long term as you will not have to make unplanned purchases during the month. You will also usually end up paying a lower price per unit for the product.

Suppliers are also willing to offer you further discounts for bulk orders or cash payments. It is your duty, as a wise consumer, to ask if this applies to you. If you are not happy, shop around (benchmark) and you will usually find another supplier willing to offer you a special deal, because you are purchasing in bulk.

8. Take advantage of loyalty discounts

There are many companies that offer consumers loyalty discounts or access to special benefits, based on past spending patterns. However, it is also a reality that many people do not take advantage of these offers.

As an added benefit, most insurance companies include value-added services, like access to a locksmith, free vehicle towing or legal advice, which comes standard with your contract.

You will save money by planning your spending in advance; being aware of the preferential rates that apply to you; and benchmarking your purchases against many suppliers.

9. Use your right brain

Be creative when it comes to spending and try to find alternatives for your spending outcome. For example, instead of buying a birthday card, create one yourself using materials purchased from a stationery or scrapbook store. Obtain a suitable poem or phrase from the Internet and add it to your card.

Food take-outs can drain money – especially if done more than twice a week, every week. Buy a cookbook or attend cooking classes and learn how to cook simple, nutritious meals.

10. Be your own financial manager

Just as a financial manager looks after a company's set of financial statements each month, so should you!

Be your own financial manager at month-end, analyzing your budget against actual amounts spent and noting the reasons for variances, both in savings and overspending.

You can also conduct mini projections to work out how much money you have saved to date, and how your current savings will accumulate in value with compounding interest by retirement.

Finally, reflect on the past month and note where you have done well on your budget, and not as well. This will help you to plan new action steps to complete the following month.

Your ultimate objective is to maintain your lifestyle expenses as per your budget, and to increase the contribution to your savings account.

The month that you start achieving this objective is the month when you know that you have disciplined yourself to budget, and to save and spend with wisdom. Your role is now to maintain this discipline.

■ Activity 6: *Become a student of life*

Learning never ends. The more you learn, the more you will be able to connect diverse topics to one another. The more you learn, the more you will grow. Below is a checklist of the things that you could do to ensure that you continue to grow.

1. Review your short-term and long-term goals regularly. Choose a new goal to achieve and put action steps in place to get it done!
2. In your business, or in the company where you work, have **Yes-energy**, and **accept challenging new assignments**. At the time, you might not know exactly how you will get the work done, but that is part of the challenge.
3. **Associate with like-minded people** who have already achieved in business and life what you are setting out to do. Regularly associating with and learning from them is like putting your hand in a jam jar. Eventually, some of that jam will stick to you!
4. **Read** at least one new book every month. After you read it, summarize it. In a separate journal, write down key learning points, along with at least three action steps that you will be taking as a consequence. This helps you to entrench knowledge. It does not matter what the book is about, as long as the content is something that you are interested in learning about.
5. **Attend a workshop or conference at least every quarter.** That will help you update your technical skills. If you walk away from a training session with at least three action steps or ideas to implement, the workshop will have been worth it!

TWO

CREATING AWARENESS
OBSERVE

> *Think highly of yourself because the world takes you at your own estimation.*
>
> **UNKNOWN**

To observe means that you notice something; that you watch carefully, or monitor closely. If you are to have control over something, it is essential that you are aware of your current reality.

Awareness precedes greatness.

Achieving greatness in life requires an assessment of your life on three levels, as listed below.

1. An evaluation of the thoughts playing on your mind.
2. An analysis of the trends that are occurring in your life.
3. An objective critique of the people with whom you associate.

It is my belief that awareness of your current reality can be analyzed in three sub-units:

1. Self-reflection
2. Self-acceptance
3. Self-belief.

Self-reflection: What do you see when you look in the mirror?

"Dineshrie, you just do not understand – my life sucks!"

These were the words uttered by one of the people I coached a few years ago. He was expressing his frustration at a challenge he was trying to overcome in his life, and he was seeking guidance from me.

The manner in which you phrase your words has a direct impact on how you feel about your life. Self-reflection is about you learning to put your current situation into perspective.

My response to him was: "Realize that your life is a continuum, with a series of ups and downs. There are times when we experience happiness. We label this as 'good'. Equally, there are times when we experience hardship, and we tend to label this as 'bad.' In order to achieve growth, you have to embrace both the good and bad in your life. So instead of saying: 'My life sucks,' say: 'This experience, event, or circumstance that I am going through sucks.' In this way, you gain control of how to deal with the situation by putting things into perspective."

FIGURE 1: *Embracing the duality of life*

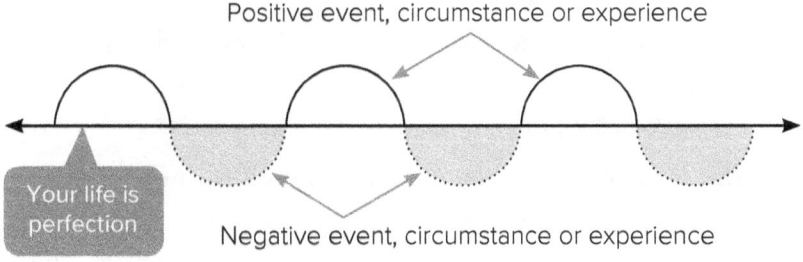

I believe that in life you attract specific events, circumstances or experiences because you are mentally able to handle them. The greater the challenge or obstacle that you learn to overcome, the greater your personal growth. The sooner you are able to deal with a challenging event, circumstance, or experience, the quicker you will grow as an individual.

Every situation is temporary: 'Good' moments fade away in time, just as 'bad' events do not last forever. You cannot savor the victory if you have not overcome the challenges.

Balanced self-reflection helps you to embrace all of your life moments. These are significant forces that shape your unique identity and build your character.

Refer to Chapter Activity 1: "Create an inspiration journal."
An inspiration journal helps you keep your life in perspective.

Self-acceptance: Are you accountable for your outcomes?

In the words of author and leadership expert Robin Sharma: "There is a disease that is plaguing society; it is called excu-situs, justi-fitus."

This reminds me that when things go wrong in my life, I need to take control of the situation and be accountable for what has happened. Whenever you try to make excuses about why something did or did not take place, or you try to justify your situation or blame other people, you essentially shift responsibility to your external environment. Shifting responsibility also shifts your ability to control the situation.

"*What have I done to contribute to this situation?*"

This is a powerful question that I ask myself whenever I am faced with a challenging situation. By asking myself this question, I am provided with insights that allow me to approach the situation differently.

By 2008, I was already a qualified Chartered Accountant registered with the South African Institute of Chartered Accountants and was now studying towards my CIMA (Chartered Institute of Management Accounting) qualification – the UK qualification.

In order to qualify and apply for admission to membership, the requirement was to read a case study on a fictional company and to complete a report that recommended strategic and operational actions, with supporting computations.

At the time of writing the exam, I held a senior role within a listed company. I was writing similar types of reports in my role. I remember thinking: "I do these types of reports all the time. There is no need for me to study extensively for this examination."

I failed my first attempt at that paper.

I could have justified my situation by saying: "It was a busy time of year at work, so I did not have more time to dedicate to my studies." I could have blamed my manager for not allowing me much study leave. Instead, I accepted my situation and re-registered for the next examination.

When, on my second attempt, I studied for that examination, I did things very differently. I analyzed past papers to identify trends in how questions were posed. I attended a board course that provided me with insights. I dedicated significant time, energy and focus to understanding how to answer those types of questions. By doing that, I found a unique way to prepare for the examination. During my studies I promised myself that, once I passed, I would become a part-time lecturer, teaching other students how to prepare for and pass that examination.

I did pass that examination, and I did become a part-time lecturer teaching my new-found examination methodology. Over a period of five years, 120 people have passed this examination using my examination techniques. Most of my students had been unsuccessful at passing this examination on their own, or had been through other board courses and not passed. When they attended my course, they passed. My pass rate averaged 80%.

I do not know what specific challenging event, circumstance, or experience you are going through in your life right now. What I do know is that once you apply the power of self-acceptance and take responsibility for your situation, you will be able to find a unique solution to your problem. Once you overcome your situation, there will be at least 5 to 10 people, if not more, who will be eager to learn from you.

Self-acceptance allows you to take back control of your situation.

Refer to Chapter Activity 2: "Change your negative beliefs into affirmations"

Self-belief: You are your biggest fan

> *The difference between the impossible and the possible lies in a person's determination.*
>
> UNKNOWN

The only thing that will remain constant in your life is change.

I am paraphrasing Greek philosopher Heraclitus. When you go through a time of change, you will be exposed to both internal and external voices. Internal voices are what you say to yourself; external voices are what other people say to you. The louder voice becomes more persuasive.

Around 2004, I made the decision to relocate from Durban to Johannesburg. Durban is a coastal city in the east of South Africa. It is my place of birth, where I grew up with my close family and friends. Johannesburg is the commercial hub of South Africa and often described as a concrete jungle.

My relocation was a career move. I knew that living and working in Johannesburg would provide me with more career options than if I stayed in Durban.

Around the time that I made the decision, two things happened simultaneously: First, I found myself unemployable. Despite being a newly-qualified Chartered Accountant, recruitment agents were hesitant to put my *curriculum vitae* forward for any listed company positions, as I needed to have articles experience with one of the bigger audit companies. When I began my articles, I had deliberately turned down articles with a bigger audit firm in order to get the all-round exposure that only a small audit firm could offer me.

In one of my first interviews with a recruitment agent in Johannesburg, I recall that person saying: "Dineshrie, I can see that you interview well, and I have no doubt that you will do well in the firm interview, but they have specifically asked for bigger audit firm experience; and for that reason, I cannot advance you further."

My heart sank. Can you imagine how I felt? After studying for four years, completing three years of articles and having one-and-a-half years of post-articles work experience as a qualified Chartered Accountant, I would not be afforded the opportunity of an interview. To make matters worse, I had paid my own flight and travel expenses from Durban to Johannesburg to attend that interview. I was on a tight budget, so this travel expense was significant to me. Faced with the same situation, I think many people would have just given up.

On the flight back from Johannesburg to Durban, I reflected on the agent's comment: "I interview well." It was all the insight and hope I needed. All I had to do was to find a recruitment agent based in Johannesburg who actually believed in my potential and who would be willing to put my *curriculum vitae* forward to the company of my choice, despite my lack of 'bigger audit firm' work experience.

One month later, I found that recruitment agent, and I was provided with the opportunity to be interviewed by the same company for which the first recruitment agent had turned me down.

At my first interview with that company, I was hired for the position. You would think that everything would be smooth sailing from here, but it was not.

Once I had accepted the position, I faced a different challenge: Leaving my family home. As the only daughter – single at the time – growing up in a traditional Indian family, it was a big leap to relocate to a new city and live on my own. The questions came from all fronts. First, from my employer at the time: "Why do you want to leave? We can promote you internally here."

Then from my family: "You are going so far away. How often will we see you? Are you sure you want to do this?"

Lastly, from my friends: "We have been friends since high school. Won't this be the end of our friendship?"

I learned a very valuable lesson at that time: During times of significant change, the voices inside your head have to be much louder than the external voices. Once people around you can see that you strongly believe in something, and that you have the conviction to make it work, their voices become subdued.

I also borrowed a lesson from my professional background as an auditor. In an audit, you:
1. Investigate the company and conduct your own tests.
2. Interview people to obtain supporting or conflicting evidence.
3. Finalize an audit report based on your test results and interviews. In your report, you state your conclusion and you stand by your statement.

You, too, can become an auditor of your own life. I do not use this term to refer to any pre-existing religious or sectarian practices, but rather to the practical process of taking stock of your life.

I believe statistics are meant to be broken down. Just because no one else has done something in your family or community does not mean that you should give up trying. Before you decide to act:
1. Conduct your own research. Investigate all aspects of your decision.
2. Interview people who have done what you are planning to do. Speak to people who have been both successful and unsuccessful.
3. Make a firm decision based on your research and interviews. Believe in yourself.

If you do not believe in your own ability to achieve something, other people will easily sway your decisions. You will then end up living your life according to others' expectations or beliefs of what you can or cannot achieve. Self-belief is about being your biggest fan.

Refer to Chapter Activity 3: "Reward yourself for your achievements."

CHAPTER 2
QUESTIONS AND ANSWERS

Q You say that everyone should be 'accountable for their outcomes,' but some of the experiences I have been through happened when I was a child. I was vulnerable. How could I have contributed to those situations?

A You are absolutely right. As a child growing up, you are vulnerable to how other people raise, nurture, and treat you. As an adult, how you reflect on those events shapes your experience of your current reality. I have met countless individuals who have been through unimaginable hardships and horrifying childhood experiences, yet have used those experiences to challenge life and beat the odds against them. They have become successful. It is about becoming a victor of your current situation instead of being a victim of your past.

Q You advise that 'I must become my biggest fan'. How do I do that when I do not like what I see in the mirror right now?

A Love is a powerful emotion. Love creates and sustains life. Love starts with yourself. I once coached a person who was very self-conscious. She complained about how her voice sounded, how she looked, and about her body shape. I could not see the things that she was complaining about. As a result of her thoughts about herself, she avoided family events, photographs, and did not like being the focus of attention. This started having an effect at work as she was not promotable because she could not work with other people. Love, gratitude, appreciation and respect for yourself are your tools to having high self-esteem. It is how I helped this particular person through what she was going through. Refer to Activities 1 and 2 at the end of this chapter for those tools.

Q I do not like change. It disrupts everything. What can I do to handle change better?

A I believe that whatever change you are having to deal with right now, you are mentally ready to handle it. In order to embrace the change, you have to adjust your attitude; change is an opportunity for you to grow. Then, take action, however small, to change. I agree that change is sometimes hard to accept, which is why I have dedicated the next chapter to this subject.

Chapter 3 deals with how to move out of your comfort levels and embrace change.

💬 Closing affirmations

1. I believe in my ability. I am my biggest fan.
2. I count my blessings; I am grateful for my life as it is.
3. I am self-driven; I am self-motivated; I am inspired.
4. I am a big-picture thinker. I am able to find the connections between different parts of life.
5. My life is perfect. Every experience is an opportunity to grow.

TAKE ACTION
CHAPTER 2 ACTIVITIES

Commitment

Observe

Nest

Tactics

Re-enforcement

Opposition

Life

■ Activity 1: *Create an inspiration journal*

Around the time that I was relocating from Durban to Johannesburg, my family home was burgled. My entire collection of sentimental jewelry was stolen. I remember having to clean up the mess after the burglars had ransacked my cupboards and strewn the contents of boxes containing my birthday cards, many of which I had kept since early childhood, all over the floor. Among the items were stubs of tickets to concerts; notes of appreciation from my work colleagues and clients; and summaries of my goals.

It took me more than four hours to put everything back in the boxes. I had spent most of that time reading the treasures I was now packing away. I was reminded of how blessed I was to have had those experiences, and to have so many people around me who loved me.

It was then that I decided to consolidate all of those inspiring pieces of information, and I created what I now call my Inspiration Journal.

I did this by opening up Word on my computer and creating one big document with sub-headings that categorized all of the inspiring notes. What follows is a list of the sections I created. When you create yours, feel free to add more categories that pertain to your life.

1. My personal goals: Long and short-term goals.
2. A summary of my hierarchy of values.
3. A daily checklist of things to do to keep me motivated.
4. My list of affirmations.
5. A collection of inspiring quotations.
6. A collection of poems that motivate me.
7. My gratitude journal.
8. A summary of all the birthday messages, well-wishes and thanks from people in my life.
9. A summary of my achievements to date, and a list of things to do, places still to see, and actions still to fulfill.
10. My financial plan.

I constantly update that Word document, and once a year I print a hard copy and carry it around with me. It has become a source of great inspiration and motivation. So now I have access to this inspiration simply by opening up a document on my computer; tabbing to a specific section and reading it, instead of scratching around in a box to find a particular item.

I encourage you to create your own inspiration journal.

■ Activity 2: *Change your negative beliefs into affirmations*

A person's assumptions, preconceptions, prejudices and core beliefs can be described as his or her truth.

These convictions are learned from early childhood and form a large part of a person's make-up. They are learned by conditioning through continuous reinforcement and repetition. This leads to certain expectations that create certain behaviors, which in turn become habits.

This is why it is important to identify any limiting beliefs you have about yourself and to redefine them as positive affirmations.

Step 1: Write down the limiting belief exactly as it is playing in your head. For example: "I am afraid of public speaking."

Step 2: Write down 10–20 reasons why the limiting belief is nonsense. Think of examples when you did speak in public. The outcome will be that you start to realize that you have been seeing yourself through one perspective only. Up until this point, you have been focusing on the negative memories. This process helps you to balance your mind again – to recognize the positive memories and to neutralize your negative perception.

Step 3: Rewrite the belief as an empowering statement. An example could be: "I am a powerful and engaging speaker." Once you define an affirmation, refine it and then regularly review it. Repeat the affirmation to yourself until it embeds within you as a new belief system.

■ Activity 3: *Reward yourself for your achievements*

Acknowledgments, whether in public or from yourself, are an important part of recognizing your success.

When you complete important milestones towards your goals, or you have accomplished something that you have not attempted before, treat yourself to a reward.

Simple reward examples could include:
1. Watching your favorite movie.
2. Treating yourself to a meal at a restaurant.
3. Buying something for yourself to acknowledge the achievement.

The reward does not have to be elaborate, as long as it feels like a reward.

THREE

CREATING AWARENESS
NEST

> *When you come to the edge of all you have known and are about to step into darkness, one of two things will happen: Either there will be something solid for you to stand on, or you will learn how to fly.*
>
> **UNKNOWN**

In this chapter, we will explore the reasons why people become complacent and how you can avoid becoming stuck in your levels of comfort.

A nest is where young birds are born and bred, until the time comes for them to fly and become independent. I use the analogy of a nest to represent your levels of comfort in all areas of life. You can identify areas in your life where you have become comfortable by asking yourself the following questions:

- In what ways have I become complacent?
- Where in my life can I improve my situation?
- What three areas of my life do I focus on within the next 12 months to radically shift my current situation?

Retaining control in your life involves constantly evaluating your existing reality and then challenging yourself by setting more audacious goals. Most people become comfortable with their existing level of performance. Life becomes easy and predictable. However, to make way for new things, life requires you to change your routine. Most people do not embrace change. If you are not embracing change, you are not moving yourself beyond your current levels of comfort and are therefore not improving your level of performance. Your next stage of growth lies just beyond your current levels of comfort.

FIGURE 2: *Growing beyond your comfort levels*

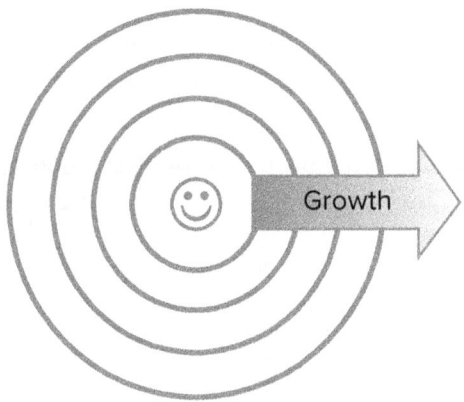

This can be illustrated by the diagram above. If your current level of comfort is at the center, and the first inner circle is your existing boundary, every time you push yourself, you will improve your level of performance. It might feel uncomfortable at first, but after experiencing something new for a period of time, your body gets used to achieving at that new level, until you again push yourself beyond that level. Keep doing this over a period of time and you will recognize the growth you have accomplished.

This principle is known as homeostasis: It is the tendency for your body to stabilize at a relative equilibrium between interdependent elements. For example, assume that you are improving your fitness levels. You hit the treadmill and push yourself beyond your current level of comfort, either in terms of time or speed. When your body (muscles and cardiovascular system) is stressed to the point where homeostasis can no longer be sustained, it responds with changes that are intended to re-establish homeostasis. Among many changes, new muscle fibers and capillaries grow. With this growth, your body has the ability to withstand the new levels of stress you place on it. It grows comfortable again. To keep improving, you constantly have to shift your levels of comfort: Run further, faster or uphill.

The reason why most people do not achieve extraordinary things is not because they are incapable of doing so, but because they have become satisfied to live in their rut of homeostasis. They do not push themselves to do the work that is required to move out of their current situation.

Most people have come to accept that 'good enough' is good enough. I am here to tell you that you have the option to do significantly better.

Refer to Chapter Activity 1: "The 'But' List."

The Peter Principle: Becoming comfortable in your career

There is a financial management theory that says: "You will rise to the level of your incompetence." This is illustrated in the diagram that follows. Each curve represents your current skills, experience, and/or qualifications. In order to progress in your career and move to a higher level, you will need to acquire a new skill, or gain more experience, or complete an additional qualification. As long as you are expanding one of these three factors, you will continue to rise. At some point, though, people plateau. They reach a limit and become comfortable with the status quo.

You will recognize these individuals as those who no longer invest in their education. They are the people who hold on to their cushy jobs. They tend to remain in those jobs for many years, not learning anything new. They are afraid of change. Change represents a threat to their current, comfortable existence. They may even become hostile and defensive to those individuals who suggest improved and creative ways of doing things: They are trying to protect their limited world.

In an ever-advancing technological era, change is inevitable. The concept of work, how we work, the ways in which we interact with each other, and how we utilize our time, is being remodeled. In this new world, it is naïve to even consider the possibility of staying comfortable for too long. If you do, you will soon have to face the imperative to move with the times or to ship out.

FIGURE 3: *The Peter Principle*

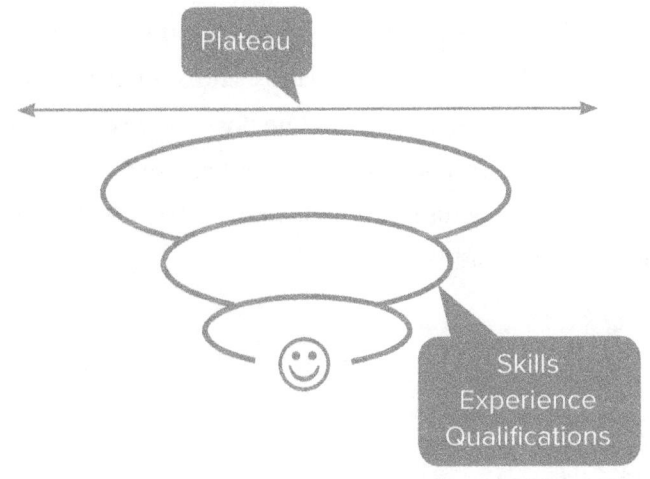

Refer to Chapter Activity 2: "List your role models."

Be wary of labeling

When you live your life according to a fixed set of rules, or a fixed schedule, you will experience a fixed set of outcomes. Fixed lifestyles attract fixed labels. When you label something, you also attach a feeling to it. Eventually you will have a reaction to the feeling and start expressing this through your emotions.

Are you familiar with comments like: "I have the Monday blues," or "Sunday evening is such a drag." These comments are examples of 'labels' that have been created as a result getting too comfortable with a fixed lifestyle.

A day is a day. It is neutral until you label it and associate a feeling to it. Comfort attracts labels.

Imagine living your life free of labels and being able to appreciate a day for exactly what it is: A blessing of time to do something meaningful. Instead of procrastinating and doing things tomorrow, you do them today.

When you push the boundaries of what you can achieve in a day, you become more proficient in how you utilize your time. You instinctively challenge existing labels and create new ones. When you challenge the labels that confine how you live and what you do with your time, you stop living according to fixed rules and start appreciating the boundless opportunities that exist to explore and enjoy life to its fullest.

Refer to Chapter Activity 3: "Time-Study Analysis."

Varying levels of change

While driving, traffic lights signal to us that green is to go; amber is to take caution; and red is to stop. Would it not be nice to have a similar 'signaling' system in life that would tell us when we are getting too complacent: A chain of warning signals that indicate to you when in life you are 'green' and growing; 'amber', or getting comfortable; and 'red', telling you to urgently change your ways.

Well you do!

Life has in place three levels of catalysts to help you enforce change. All you have to do is follow the signs.

LEVEL 1: You realize the need to change, and you make the decision to do so (*green light*).

LEVEL 2: You are stubborn, or living in blissful ignorance about what is happening around you, so a friend or family member tries to convince you to change (*amber light*).

LEVEL 3: You attract a humbling event, circumstance, or experience that forces you to change (*red light*).

Have you ever heard of someone who was unhappy in their job for years, but after being retrenched, took their pension and started a successful business? Or the person who was unhappy in their relationship? Despite everyone telling them that their partner was not good for them, they stayed in the relationship only to find out that their partner was cheating on them? Or think of the person who enjoyed a life of partying, alcohol and excessive eating, only to find themselves in life-threatening circumstances that ultimately radically changed their behavior.

All the scenarios above: The 'retrenchment,' 'cheating,' and 'life-threatening circumstances,' are examples of Level 3 catalytic events.

In my life, numerous Level 3 catalytic events have occurred. The first was failing my Board Examination towards becoming a Chartered Accountant. I could not get over the fact that I had failed – again. I should have been able to get over that failure quickly, but I just could not. I got to a stage where I took down all my undergraduate and postgraduate certificates from the wall because I felt empty without that particular certificate. Family and work colleagues tried to get me out of my funk by telling me that it would be okay and that I would pass next time. Nothing helped me.

About three weeks later, I was involved in a car accident. It was my fault. I had been feeling morose and was not focused on the road when I drove into an oncoming vehicle. Thankfully, neither of us was injured. Our vehicles were not as lucky. I remember thinking: "Dineshrie, you are such an idiot – you could have lost your life, or even worse, you could have injured innocent people." This Level 3 event prompted me to change my attitude.

That example we discussed earlier about the person being unhappy in their relationship only to find out that their partner was having an affair... well that was me, too! I will tell you more about this experience in a later chapter.

You will attract Level 3-type events when you have become too comfortable in your situation and you are failing to read the signs around you. When you are in that state, you ignore the messages from your family and friends and put on a front that everything is working well, even though it is not.

Why do this to yourself?

Time is so precious and fleeting. Why await a Level 3-type event to spur you to action? There are signs of change all around you. Life provides you with its own version of a robot signal. Be attuned to these signals and act quickly to get out of your comfort level. When you do this, you will take back control of your life.

Nature's lesson on overcoming comfort

I am a self-confessed nerd, and am happy to retain this title. I have stacks of books, magazines and videos with which I keep myself entertained. My favorite television channel is National Geographic. I love learning about the world, its people, and the universe. I enjoy finding correlations between the natural world and our human existence.

I once watched a documentary about the wood duck, which is a species of perching duck found in North America. The female duck makes its nest high up in a tree, near water. To protect its eggs, the nest can be as high as 15–20m above the ground. This species of duck can lay 7 to 15 eggs at a time.

When the ducklings are ready to leave the nest, the mother first flies to the ground and calls to its ducklings. One at a time, the little birds make the courageous leap from high up in the tree into the soft leaves at the bottom, on the ground. Some of the chicks jump on their own; others jump together. The mother continues to call to her chicks until they have all jumped. Once reunited, they merrily waddle off to the pond.

As I watched this, I was reminded of what it takes to 'leave your nest' and do something out of your comfort zone.

1. You need a mentor; someone to guide you along and encourage you to take that leap. For the wood duck, it was the mother who first made it to the ground and then called out to her chicks to join her.
2. No one forced the chicks to jump. When they were ready, they leaped in the air. The lesson is that you can have all the best coaches in the world, but they cannot force you to take action. Only you can do that.
3. The most difficult step to take is the first one. Once you take the leap and prove to yourself that you can do it, the second attempt is a little easier.

Step out of your nest. It is part of life's plan to bring out the best in you.

> *No one can predict to what heights you can soar, even you will not know until you spread your wings.*
>
> **UNKNOWN**

Thoughts are powerful forces that control how you feel and act. Next, we look at how your mind works and ways to control your experience by changing your thought process.

CHAPTER 3

QUESTIONS AND ANSWERS

Q What if I have a medical condition that makes it challenging for me to pursue my dream and career ambitions?

A Stephen Hawking was an English theoretical physicist, cosmetologist and author. He had a rare early onset form of motor neuron disease that gradually paralyzed him over the decades. In spite of his loss of speech, Hawking found ways to communicate through a speech generating device. He made profound contributions in his area of specialty despite his medical condition. I believe that when you have a strong enough will, there is always a way.

Q Is it okay to stay in my current 'cushy' position, but constantly educate myself and improve on the work methods and processes in my role?

A Yes, absolutely. When you are constantly learning and challenging how things are done, you are growing. You might be in the same position, but you are committed to change and embracing new ideas. The concern I have is if you are in the same position for many years and are not improving in the role in any way.

Q I sometimes feel so alone in my thoughts, as everyone expects me to be the perfect role model for the family. If I am supposed to be the role model, who do I look to for guidance?

A I hear you! Firstly, change your thoughts. You are certainly not alone in what you are going through. Secondly, no one is perfect. Tell people you are not perfect, and do not act as if you are. Humble yourself and acknowledge that you do not have all the answers. Help comes when you ask for it.

🗨 Closing affirmations

1. I have unique talents and skills to offer. I love and appreciate my uniqueness.
2. Every day, in every way, I am moving up my own learning curve.
3. The more often I do something, the better I become at it.
4. Change is the medium through which I grow and prosper.
5. Feedback from other people is the water that feeds my growth.

TAKE ACTION
CHAPTER 3 ACTIVITIES

Commitment

Observe

Nest

Tactics

Re-enforcement

Opposition

Life

■ Activity 1: *The 'but' list*

Make a list of all the things you've always wanted to do, but never got a chance to because you said: "But…". For example: "I would like to go to a movie, *but* I am too busy," or "I always wanted to try surfing, *but* I do not have anyone to join me."

The word 'but' has a psychological impact. It creates an invisible barrier that prevents you from doing what you would like to do.

Now, review your list and replace 'but' with 'and'.

The word 'and' extends the statement from an outright 'no' answer to a possibility. Where there is a possibility, there is still hope for you to take action.

The word 'but' is limiting. The word 'and' is limitless.

■ Activity 2: *List your role models*

When you make a decision to do something new, it helps to know that there are other people somewhere in the world who have accomplished similar goals to those you have set. They may not be exactly the same goals, but the form will be similar. Find these role models. Study and analyze their methods. Learn from them. Become inspired by their actions, because if they can do great things, so can you. Limitations exist only in your mind.

■ Activity 3: *Time-study analysis*

Conduct a time-study analysis of how you currently spend your waking hours, from Monday to Sunday. Write down everything you do, including the times that you eat; how long you spend in traffic; what time you go to sleep; and how you spend your weekend.

This analysis will provide you with insight into how you can change your schedule or eliminate low-priority tasks. In so doing, you will free up time to implement new changes or actions in your life.

FOUR

CREATING AWARENESS
TACTICS

> *You will find, as you look back upon your life, that the moments that stand out, the moments when you have really lived, are the moments when you have done things in the spirit of love.*
>
> **HENRY DRUMMOND**

Taking action

Tactics are plans or actions to achieve a particular result. Every action, outcome and experience starts with a thought. Someone thought about building the tallest structure in the world. Someone thought about space travel and putting a man on the moon. Someone thought about creating technology that would allow people across the world to speak to each other and share memories in the form of videos, pictures and voice recordings through mobile applications.

Everything begins with a thought.

The more you think about something, the more you give it focus and provide it with life. Thoughts that get played over and over again in your head soon become the words you utter to other people. You attach feelings to words and give them meaning. Once a thought means something to you, you will act on how you feel. Your actions become your reality.

Energy takes on various forms. Your thoughts are a form of energy. Energy is also transferable from one form to another. If you are thinking about your life in a negative way – as if your life is an enemy – then you have it wrong. The way you are thinking is the real enemy. You have the power to think of any thought. No one gives you a list of thoughts to think about every morning. If you want to change your experiences in life, start by changing your thoughts.

Refer to Chapter Activity 1: "Consciously change your thoughts."

Understand how your brain works

A few years ago, I became fascinated with trying to understand how our brains work. I believe we have unlimited power in the form of unutilized brain capacity. My background in auditing has taught me that if you can understand how a system works, you will better maximize its potential. The subject of mind control is an area of study that even scientists in this field of learning have not yet mastered. They are constantly learning new ways to tap brain capacity. As a consequence, this area of specialism is also an ongoing study for me.

What I have learned, which is agreed upon by many researchers, is that in the area of our thinking, there are three parts of the brain that can help you to understand how you think and react: The thalamus, the neocortex and the amygdala.

The thalamus is the part of the brain that receives all the sensory signals: What you see, hear, taste, touch and smell. From the thalamus, synaptic connections route this information to the neocortex – the thinking part of the brain. This part of the brain decides what to do with the signals. For instance, you see a vehicle on the freeway moving into your lane (the thalamus collected this information). You then quickly swerve to the side to avoid a possible collision (your neocortex made this decision).

A neuroscientist by the name of Joseph Ledoux conducted research on the brain in the area of emotions. He found that there was a very small, but significant synaptic connection between the thalamus and the amygdala, which is the part of the brain in charge of your feelings. Because of this connection, your amygdala can sometimes over-react, based on the sensory signals it receives. This is called an emotional hijacking. So, if you thought about the car swerving into your lane, your amygdala could have over-reacted and made you become emotional. You may have panicked and screamed, not reacting fast enough to avoid a collision.

I have found this information very insightful when it comes to managing my emotions on a daily basis. If you become highly emotional about something, your amygdala is doing the thinking for you. If you are able to stay calm and think rationally, your neocortex is doing the thinking for you.

Yes, there are times when you need to be emotional, but would you prefer to be the person who has constant emotional outbursts, or the person who thinks and behaves diplomatically and calmly? I am sure you would agree that being calm and rational is the way to go.

Refer to Chapter Activity 2: "Give your mind 'challenges' to solve."

A way to control your emotions

We live in a Google world. If you ask most people something they are unsure of, a likely response would be: "Hang on a moment, let me just Google that…"

Using this example, do you agree that what you type into Google, you will most likely find? As an example, if you type into Google: "Why can't a 35-year-old woman lose weight?" (This was me a few years ago), you would find a host of blog postings, articles and statistics validating why a 35-year-old woman cannot lose weight. You will get responses that include references to your blood-type; your age; your metabolism; your family history; your history of being overweight; your diet… and so the list goes on. However, if you type into Google: "How can a 35-year-old woman lose weight?" I guarantee you that you will get a completely different set of responses.

Your brain is like a Google search engine. At any moment in time, you are either asking yourself a question or making a statement. I need you to observe if the question or statement you are making is of a poor quality. If so, it will keep you in 'hijack' mode. If your question or statement is of a high quality, it will provide you with solutions and actions to your problem.

Let's say, for example, you are driving to your friend's house and you get lost. Your phone is dead, so you do not have a GPS to help you. It is getting dark and you find yourself on a narrow, potholed road. It then starts to rain. A poor-quality statement would be: "Oh my word, I am so lost – I am going to get stuck here," or "I have no idea where I am right now, I might damage my tyres in one of these potholes."

These thoughts are examples of your amygdala going into hijack mode. These statements do not help you stay calm and focused to find solutions.

Now, imagine if you had instead said to yourself: "Calm down, I will get you out of this area," or "Slow down, put your lights on, watch out for those potholes." Perhaps you may have just said: "I will just back-track and find the nearest garage to get directions and call for help."

These are examples of good-quality statements in which the thinking part of the brain is being used to help you to stay calm and rational.

A few years ago, I heard businessman and motivational speaker T. Harv Ecker speak at a conference. Something he said stuck with me: "What you focus on expands." This makes so much sense when it comes to understanding how our brains work. If you are going to focus on the negative aspects of a situation, the negative part will get bigger. If you focus on the positive, the positive part gets bigger. Empower your brain with good-quality questions and statements. What you focus on expands.

Refer to Chapter Activity 3: "Practice single-tasking."

Gain perspective

Life is too short to worry about little things that have no meaning in the long term. Every day you will be exposed to all types of events, circumstances and experiences.

Ask yourself, "Will this matter to me one year from today?"

If not, do not allocate any more energy to the matter. Focus on things that add long-term meaning and value to your life.

Refer to Chapter Activity 4: "Clean and organize your environment."

Trust your intuition

Neocortex, rational thinking is part of your conscious brain, but there is thinking that stems from your sixth sense, also known as your intuition.

I believe that you can learn to trust and be guided by your intuition. This takes time and patience. It also means that you learn how to receive feedback from the world around you: Both from people and from nature.

This is how I listen to and trust my intuition: If something does not feel right, I feel it in my body. I get a hollow feeling in my stomach. My gut tells me that something is wrong, and I should not go ahead with a decision. Conversely, when I have a peaceful feeling in my chest, I know a decision makes sense.

I remember when I bought my first home. After spending weeks looking at houses online and physically viewing places, I walked through the door of the house that I eventually purchased and knew it was going to be the place I called home. I could see myself in that space; I felt that the decision was the right one to make.

My intuition speaks to me in my dreams. If, upon waking, I have a thought that is playing over in my head, and it sounds like someone is shouting at me, I pay attention to those thoughts.

This book that you are holding in your hands is the third edition. I recall being on a flight from Johannesburg to Durban to visit my family two years after I published the second edition. I fell asleep on the plane. When the air steward announced that it was time to prepare to land, I woke up thinking: "Rewrite the book." It was this nagging thought led me to this third edition, in which I have updated the content and restructured the book's message.

I pay attention to opportunities that open up to me. If the same type of opportunity keeps presenting itself to me, I take notice. When I started my business, I used to introduce myself as a life coach and offered very different services from what I offer today. In spite of offering life coaching programs, I was constantly being asked to develop training interventions for leaders in business. Today, leadership development is my area of specialty.

If I decide to do something my way, and it is different from how other people would advise me to do it, but I feel confident in my decision anyway, I know that this is my instinct, saying: "Don't worry about those nay-sayers; do it your way and show them how it is done."

A few years ago, I proposed a training intervention for a big, listed company. In the past, this program was typically run in smaller groups of 8 to 12 delegates. I came up with a way to implement it for 60 delegates. There was a lot of negativity around my approach and its effectiveness. At the same time, I trusted my instinct and implemented the program. Today, the manner in which I run this particular program has become an example to others on how to run it. I also had the opportunity to train many other trainers in my approach and methodology.

Finally, I have learned to build in 'me-time', which is basically rest and relaxation. I find that in the quieter moments I am blessed with clarity of thought and creative solutions to my everyday challenges.

Refer to Chapter Activity 5: "Find time for quiet reflection."

> *You are never given a dream without also being given the power to make it true.*
>
> **RICHARD BACH**

Mental readiness

I believe that you will attract a challenge that you are mentally ready to handle. The blessing of growth comes in the form of a challenge. When you view challenges in this way, your thinking in how to deal with them changes significantly. You become assertive and confident.

In the movie *Evan Almighty*, Morgan Freeman plays the role of God, guiding the main character to fulfill a task. What follows is a quote from the movie:

"Let me ask you something. If someone prays for patience, you think God gives them patience? Or does he give them the opportunity to be patient? If he prayed for courage, does God give him courage, or does he give him opportunities to be courageous? If someone prayed for the family to be closer, do you think God zaps them with warm, fuzzy feelings, or does he give them opportunities to love each other?"

This statement is a reminder that opportunities do not always present themselves in a positive way. You have attracted a certain opportunity for a reason. Embrace the challenge. Say to yourself: "I am ready to handle this challenge," and then dedicate all of your mental resources to dealing with it.

Steve Jobs once said: "You can only connect the dots looking back." Only once you have been through a challenge will you understand the significance it has had in your life. Openly embrace your challenges.

Shifting your paradigm – the process of transmutation

When I launched the second edition of this book, I conducted conferences and book launches in various South African cities. As part of that campaign, I had professional photographers take pictures of the event for my own marketing and use on my websites.

After the second book launch in Durban, I received the pictures from my photographer. I remember being so horrified, as I looked terribly overweight. I remember thinking to myself: "Dineshrie, you are such a hypocrite! Here you are writing a book about looking after yourself and you cannot even do it for yourself!"

In my (emotional) defense, about 10 months earlier, I had injured the meniscus on my right knee. That injury restricted movement and I had gained a lot of weight during that time.

However, the rational side of my brain knew that for many years I had been trying to lose weight and had been unsuccessful. I started to ask myself: "Why do I achieve success in work and in education, but when it comes to exercise, I remain such a failure?"

I attained three of my qualifications while working full-time and studying part-time. Considering that, I started to analyze the factors that led to my success in my education, and how I could gain insights that I could apply to an area I was not good at – health and fitness.

I began adopting a process called transmutation: Taking one form and applying it to another. This has become a powerful technique that I use in my individual coaching sessions with clients. Below is an illustration of how to do this for yourself. I have used my education-fitness example to illustrate this for you.

Take a page and draw a line down its center.

On the left side, think of an area of your life that you are currently good at. On the right side, think of an area of your life in which you seek improvement. On the left side, write down all the factors that make you successful. On the right side, think of how you can take those factors and apply them to the area of life you are seeking to improve. To illustrate how you could use the process of transmutation, I have reconstructed the outcome of my own exercise within the table that follows.

AREA OF LIFE CURRENTLY ACHIEVING SUCCESS	AREA OF LIFE CURRENTLY NOT ACHIEVING GOALS
My example: Education [You insert your area] [Write down actions that you take to achieve success in this area] My example is listed below	**My example: Fitness** [You insert your area] [Write down application of the principles from your area of success] My example is listed below
Before I study, I conduct **research** on the modules. I get hold of past examination papers. I know in advance which topics are commonly asked, and I have pass-rate statistics to guide me on areas of focus.	I can conduct **research** on the area of fitness. I can research diet and nutrition, and the fitness programs of different celebrities. I can understand how to eat according to my blood type.
I have a detailed study **timetable** and schedule of examination questions to attempt. I study 6 days in a week, with an off-day. This regimen is not negotiable.	I can obtain the gym **timetable** and schedule of classes. I will train 6 days a week, regardless of how tired I am. I will make the effort to attend a class. This is not negotiable.
I tell people that I am studying and to not feel bad if I am unable to socialize with them. I have an examination to pass.	**I tell people** that I am on a strict diet and not to feel bad if I do not eat their sweet desserts.
I **repeatedly** attempt a question until I gain at least 75% of the marks. I will continue to attempt a question until I feel confident to answer it.	I will **repeatedly** attend a gym class if I find I am weak in that area of fitness. For example: I will continue to go to an abs class until my core is strong again.

AREA OF LIFE CURRENTLY ACHIEVING SUCCESS	AREA OF LIFE CURRENTLY NOT ACHIEVING GOALS
I seek out **role models** who have completed this examination and ask them for advice on how to succeed at this examination.	I will seek out **role models** in the area of fitness. I will read their biographies. This will inspire me to achieve the same results for myself.
I will align myself to **coaches** in the form of lecturers and tutors who can teach me the theory.	I will align myself to a **coach** in the form of a personal trainer to help me achieve my fitness goals.
Once I pass, I will **reward** myself with a gift of my choice.	**Rewards** for reaching my fitness milestones will come in the form of upgraded fitness shoes, clothing, and training gadgets.
I will take vitamin **supplements** to help me sustain long hours of studying.	I will invest in **supplements** to help me sustain pre- and post-workout sessions.
Tests leading up to the final examination are like **mini-challenges** to test my performance. The results of these tests will provide me with feedback on areas to improve.	I will start competing in outdoor events that will be my **mini-challenges**, and will serve to test my strength and endurance. I will use my level of performance as feedback on areas of improvement.

I believe that embedded in each one of you is an unconscious 'success formula' that will help you achieve greatness in your life. You are unique in your experiences, upbringing and thinking. It is this uniqueness that allows you to do things differently.

Using the power of transmutation, you can significantly shift your thinking and uncover your unique success formula.

Let us now explore the concept of relationships and the contribution that other people make in your life.

CHAPTER 4

QUESTIONS AND ANSWERS

Q I do follow the idea of being rational rather than emotional. So, are you saying that from here on, I should not get emotional and only think rational thoughts?

A Oh goodness no! As much as I know and teach this principle, I still do get emotional at times and encourage you to do the same. You need to have the emotional outburst so that negative energy is not being stored within your bodily system. What I have shared with you is a technique to not remain emotionally hijacked for days and months on end, as doing so wastes valuable time and energy. It also damages your relationships with other people. This is a technique for controlling your emotions so that you can logically think of creative solutions for your unique challenge.

Q You say that we should 'openly embrace challenges'. My challenge is too big – I can't do this alone. What do I do?

A Big challenges require a big shift in your level of thinking, and an even bigger network of people to help you to overcome them. Achieving big dreams and overcoming huge life obstacles feels more rewarding when you enlist the help of other people.

Q Can the process of transmutation be applied to any situation in any area of life?

A Most definitely, yes! I have used the process with my own delegates, clients and students and helped them to gain insights. I can confirm that this principle can be applied to any situation. Try it for yourself and you will see its magic!

🗨 Closing affirmations

1. I attract opportunities that I am mentally able to handle.
2. I am unique. I am confident. I use my personal success formula in all areas of my life.
3. I am guided by my instincts. I listen to my instincts.
4. I will focus on matters that have long-term meaning for me and let go of everything else.
5. Every step I take is a step taken in a forward direction.

TAKE ACTION
CHAPTER 4 ACTIVITIES

Commitment

Observe

Nest

Tactics

Re-enforcement

Opposition

Life

■ Activity 1: *Consciously change your thoughts*

Over a period of a week, be aware of the types of thoughts you are thinking. Are they poor-quality, amygdala-hijack-mode thoughts that make you more emotional and immobilized? Or are they rational, solution-seeking-type thoughts?

As soon as you observe that you are thinking a poor-quality thought, change it to something that either keeps you positive, or helps you seek solutions. After you have done this for a week, assess how you feel, as well as the type of accomplishments that you achieved for that week.

Set a goal to consciously change your thoughts in the second week. Reassess your accomplishments at the end of that week. Continue to do this until you get to a stage where you are aware of your thoughts and you can quickly shift your thinking to more affirmative, action-orientated thoughts.

■ Activity 2: *Give your mind 'challenges' to solve*

Instead of labeling an event or circumstance as a 'problem', rephrase it to a 'challenge'. The word 'problem' sounds so heavy and burdensome, but a 'challenge' sounds like a creative puzzle for you to solve. I would personally prefer a creative puzzle to solve than a heavy burden to deal with.

Provide your mind with a specific challenge to solve by telling yourself exactly what you are looking for. Let us take a simple example to illustrate. Let us assume that you are thinking of changing your cooking menu for the week and you say to yourself, "I am looking for creative ways to cook healthy meals this week with limited ingredients." In order to help your mind find a creative solution, feed it with facts; figures; research; stories; visuals; and any other information to help you find a solution. Think of this process as feeding information into a powerful super-computer. Then, do something completely different, do not think of solving for the problem.

Instead, go and watch a movie; socialize with your friends; sleep and rest. Your mind is now simmering on the information you have provided to it. Creative ideas will surface to your conscious brain when you least expect it. Have a pen and paper on hand to note down the ideas that come to you. Type out the idea onto your mobile device. Finally, take action on your idea.

■ Activity 3: *Practice single-tasking*

Multi-tasking is a myth. If someone says that they are good at multi-tasking, what they really mean is that they've become good at quickly switching from one task to another.

When you focus intently on one task at a time, you shut out outside noise and disturbances and allocate significant thinking power to completing that single task.

Every day, practice single-tasking by blocking out time in your schedule to focus only on completing a particular task. Group similar items together – like making phone calls, or completing your administration. Doing this increases the power of your focus.

■ Activity 4: *Clean and organize your environment*

The mind thinks better in an ordered environment. When you surround yourself with clutter, you are unable to think clearly. It may even take you longer to find things. A chaotic environment leads to chaotic thoughts. Instead of using your time to think efficiently and be productive, you lose time because you are not focused.

Clean and organize all of your spaces. Create order and structure in your vehicle; computer folders; clothing cupboards; cosmetic and grooming products; work-space and bookshelves – any space that is your own. Organize and tidy up.

■ **Activity 5:** *Find time for quiet reflection*

During the day, your mind is flooded with information. As long as you are awake, your mind is absorbing and processing information.

Consider the range of information we are exposed to on a daily basis:
- Television
- Radio
- Waking up to an alarm clock or radio
- Hosting and participating in meetings
- Holding discussions with other people
- Responding to emails
- Updating social media content
- Reading text messages
- Reading various forms of marketing, billboards and advertisements during the day.

During this time, your brain is working at both a conscious and unconscious level. When you calm your thinking enough to be able to pause for a moment and be still, it helps you to reduce your anxiety and stress. It can also help you to think more.

A simple meditation technique

Sit comfortably in a chair. Ensure that both feet are flat on the ground and not crossed. Keep your hands to your sides or on your lap, and relax your shoulder muscles. Start by taking control of your breathing. Breathe in for a count of four, then breathe out for a count of 12. As you breathe out, imagine that you are expelling every last bit of air out of your lungs.

Practice deep breathing for 3 minutes.

After 3 minutes, close your eyes and focus on your next thought. You will most likely be so conscious of your surroundings that you actually do not think of anything.

While in this state, be aware of the sounds around you. Maintain your deep breathing.

Stay in this state for another 2 to 7 minutes.

FIVE

CREATING AWARENESS
RE-ENFORCEMENT

> *You are the same today as you are going to be five years from now, except for two things: The people with whom you associate and the books you read.*
>
> **CHARLES JONES**

Our binding forces

The Cradle of Humankind, about 90 minutes outside of Johannesburg, South Africa, is the world's richest hominid site and contains around 40% of the world's human ancestor fossils. You can only but feel awe when visiting this place, as it becomes so evident how much we have evolved as humans.

When you enter the site and its museum, a plaque reads:
We are diverse species, bound by nine common characteristics that make us human:

1. *Our complex brain*
2. *Our jaws and diet*
3. *A history of peopling the world*
4. *The advanced ability to make tools*
5. *The ability to make and control fire*
6. ***Our preference for living with others***
7. *An exceptional capacity for creativity*
8. *Our ability to walk upright (Bipedalism)*
9. *The ability to use complex language to communicate.*

When I read this, I was drawn to point 6: Our preference for living with others. If this is a fundamental characteristic of humans, then we should learn not only how to live with each other, but also how to help each other on our respective life journeys.

Refer to Chapter Activity 1: "Engage in acts of selflessness."

You become that with whom you associate

I believe that relationships are the cement that reinforce the bricks of your goals.

You have goals that you strive towards. In attaining your goals, you can either choose to do it on your own, or you can surround yourself with people who can help you achieve them faster. If you consider your top achievements in your life to date, can you remember if you achieved them on your own, or if you had a network of people to support you? I am sure it was the latter.

Now think about a major goal you would like to achieve within the next two to three years. In order to achieve it, you will likely need 50 to 100 people to help you. Most of these people will be new to your network. Some of them will be individuals who refer you to someone else in their network. A few of these people will be in your existing network. Are you on track to meet 50 to 100 people?

When you are challenging and pushing yourself beyond what you are capable of doing, it is imperative to surround yourself with people who have already achieved similar goals for themselves. You might be one of the few people in your circle of family and friends who has embarked on that journey, so you will have to consciously seek out people beyond your existing network who can support, mentor and guide you. If you do not do this, you could very easily get drawn back into the life of comfort and stability that is so familiar to your existing network of family and friends.

Seek out a mentor and coach to guide you. A mentor is someone you can look up to as a role model. A mentor can be someone you know, or someone you follow from a distance, like a well-known public figure. A coach is someone who is constantly at your side, correcting your actions and providing you with ongoing support and feedback. A coach will offer more direct support to you.

In addition, seek to include at least one close friend with whom you can speak: Someone who understands your journey, and whom you trust wholeheartedly. Finally, enlist in your network at least one person who is going to act as your agent; someone who talks to other people on your behalf and who effectively creates opportunities for you. That person is your rainmaker.

Refer to Chapter Activity 2: "How to find your mentor."

I have been following the remarkable story of Usain Bolt, the fastest man on Earth. When he shares his life story, he talks about the three people closest to him. The first is his coach. Despite his success and ability to enlist the help of any coach in the world, Usain Bolt remained with his original coach. The second is his agent, who helps him with his public relations and marketing efforts. The third is his best friend. That person is by his side when he travels. It is someone he trusts and with whom he can be himself. As far as role models go, Usain Bolt is a record-breaker, so when he competes, he always attempts to better his last performance.

When creating your close mastermind group, think triad: Coach, friend, agent.

The redwood tree

As far as record-breakers go, in the forest you will find one in the form of a tree called a Redwood. This tree is described as the 'ancient giant of the forest'. The redwood can grow to a height of 113m, with a diameter of 3–9m. This tree species can be found in three parts of the world: Northern California, a strip in Nevada, and a remote valley in China.

I use this tree as a metaphor for how we grow in life. In order for the redwood tree to grow and tower above all the others, it needs to shed its leaves at the bottom. Once it has shed those leaves, it will develop new branches higher up, with new leaves, and so the process of growth continues.

In life, think of yourself as a redwood tree. In order to grow and tower above the rest, you, too, are required to shed leaves in the form of family and friends who no longer support or share your values. If you continue to associate with people who do not support you, it will be easy for them to attack your new values; become jealous of your success; or just not be able to relate intellectually to what you are saying or doing.

I know this. I have experienced it for myself.

While still a student at university, I had a lot of friends. We partied and experimented with alcohol and cigarettes together. Years later, after I had qualified and no longer smoked cigarettes or drank alcohol, I found that when I connected with these friends, we no longer had anything to talk about. In the past, the focus had been on drinking and partying, but I was no longer that person.

I remember leaving a particular function early. I realized that when you try to associate with people who do not share your intellectual values, it is easier for them to bring you down to their level, instead of connecting with you at your level. I learned to shed my leaves in the form of friends and family (except my immediate family members), who no longer supported me. So, I made new friends, who are now my extended family.

I joined clubs and associations that were filled with like-minded individuals; people who shared my goals. I started following certain people on social media, and through their books, conferences, webinars, newsletters and articles, I associate with them. I make a point of investing in my continuous education, and I read extensively, often changing the author or genre of what I read. I constantly evaluate my network and make changes accordingly.

Refer to Chapter Activity 3: "Travel and enhance your world view."

Practice deliberate Seva

In Sanskrit, Seva means 'selfless service', or work performed without any thought of reward or repayment. In ancient India, Seva was believed to help one's spiritual growth while simultaneously contributing to the improvement of the community.

When you give your time, service and support without expectation, there is no obligation for the other party to return the favor. There is no need to keep track of who helped whom. There is no need to have petty discussions that sound like: "I helped you on this occasion, next time it is your turn," or "You owe me a favor."

Seva is also about giving without expecting any praise for your efforts. If you would like to donate to a worthy cause, do so anonymously. Seva is not a once-off event during the year. It is not a marketing campaign to show how moral you are. Seva is an everyday activity.

Refer to Chapter Activity 4: "Perform random acts of Seva."

Spotlight or shadow?

We live in a world where co-operation and competition co-exist in harmony. Co-operation creates teams that can achieve more than individual effort. Competition is the fuel for creativity and innovation. It allows us to constantly improve how we live.

The lines between competition and co-operation can be blurred at times, especially when we are in the company of people who are achievers in their own right. Check yourself and your reaction to these people. Be sincerely happy for them. Support what they are doing. It is so easy to slip into competition-mode and say things like: "Oh wow, is that what you are doing right now. I am doing the same…" The ego in you wants to compare, compete and overshadow the other person's success. Bring out your altruistic side and let them have the spotlight they deserve. Instead, say: "That is wonderful news, I am happy for you, tell me more…"

Treat people as you would like to be treated. Let other redwood trees have their turn in the spotlight. Respect is mutual.

Refer to Chapter Activity 5: "Look after something living."

You are more than how you behave

I have learned to separate a person's behavior from the person. I usually find that the way in which a person behaves and appears on the outside is a deeper, more complex cry for help. If you take the time to show empathy, patience, and understanding, you will learn the real reason for their behavior. Drivers of 'unacceptable' behavior are usually linked to unresolved pain, hardship and challenges.

Although you cannot force someone to openly share their true feelings with you; you can be patient, and listen with empathy. You can still offer to help and support them when they are ready to talk to you. Sometimes, all a person needs is the thought that they are not alone and there are people around them who are willing to help them.

There is a Buddhist teaching that says: "When the student is ready, the teacher will appear." Give the person time to internalize what they are going through. When they are ready, they will share their concerns with you.

Refer to Chapter Activity 6: "Make the first contact."

> *People are more important than things.*
>
> **RANDY PAUSCH**

Presence versus presents

In your role of helping and supporting others, the little things you consistently do usually mean more than elaborate shows of affection. Are you the person who is quick to respond to a missed call? Are you the person who takes hours, or even days, to return a phone call? Do you remember key events, like anniversaries, birthdays and special moments? Do you arrive on time for special occasions, social outings, or even casual events? Little things are not that little. They are actually big factors when it comes to creating a perception of how a person remembers your relationship with them.

I learned this lesson a few years ago. I schedule regular visits to see my family in Durban. In the past, I often used to buy presents for my family members. At some point, my father opened a gift that I had bought for him and, after thanking me, said: "You do not need to buy me gifts every time you visit. Your presence here with me is more important than your presents." He repeated that several times to ensure that I got the message. I got the message.

Those words taught me that your presence, and being able to share your time with people you love and care for, is more important than anything of material value that you can give to them.

Can you remember what you bought someone for their birthday or a special occasion five years ago? Or do you more vividly recall how you spent the day with them? Over a period of time, gifts can break; they can get used up or worn out, but the memories of your presence and love are timeless.

> *People care about you when you care about them. It is not about how interesting you are, it is about how interested you are in them.*
>
> **UNKNOWN**

Living and loving without regret

We often wait until it is too late to tell a person how grateful we are for the role they have played in our lives. Many people live their lives avoiding other people whom they no longer speak to because of disagreements or misunderstandings. In such situations, the person who suffers the most is the person who carries the grudge.

Life is too short to walk around with grudges, or to delay your appreciation and gratitude for people you care for.

In June 2015, my parents flew from Durban to Johannesburg to be with me. It was Father's Day weekend, and I decided to do something different for my father. I took the time to put together a collage of pictures of myself growing up, and specifically included pictures of my father. Each picture depicted a moment in time that held a special memory for me. I wrote a detailed letter of gratitude and appreciation to him, thanking him for instilling in me the values and beliefs that helped me to become the person I am today.

I am really glad I did that. My mum told me that when they returned home, my father kept that card in the breakfast area and that he read it in the mornings.

Three weeks later, my father passed away.

Even though I am a public speaker, at his funeral I did not feel the need to deliver a eulogy. Firstly, I was too emotional to speak, but I also had the comfort of knowing that whatever I had to say, I had done it in person. He knew how much I appreciated and loved him.

Think about the last time you wrote a letter of heartfelt gratitude to someone you care about. I am not referring to quick text messages or short emails, or the quick verbal: "thank you" or "I love you." I am talking about a detailed and sincere letter of appreciation, specifying what the person means to you.

We often wait until its too late.

While showing gratitude and appreciation to someone you love and care for might be easy, it becomes harder when you have to let go of relationships that do not end well.

Two years after my father passed on, I found out that my life partner was cheating on me. Until that point, we had been in a relationship for just under 10 years. It broke my heart to find out about the affair in the manner I did. Within a week of finding out, I ended the relationship. There were no arguments, no fights and no more blame. There just existed a calm discussion about how it was time to end our relationship and to go on with our lives separately.

When he left, I packaged together all the sentimental items I could no longer bear to keep, including all the teddy bears and rings that he had given me. The rings represented a commitment to me that had been broken. The sentimental items no longer had meaning for me as they were a reminder of the trust that had been broken. In spite of how I felt at the time, I also included a letter of gratitude, thanking him for his support and the role that he played in my life while we were together. It was hard at first to write this letter, but when I focused on the reasons why I stayed in a relationship with him, I was able to write that letter. I am glad I did that. It allowed me to move on with my life without anger, hostility or hurt. All that was left was an acceptance of my new reality.

When you live your life without regret or resentment, and appreciate all forms of relationships, you are able to feel grateful for the role that people play in your life. Every person that comes into your life does so for a reason. By harnessing the power of appreciation, gratitude and love, those reasons become clearer to you.

Refer to Chapter Activity 7: "Write thank you letters."

Next, we will talk about the big topic of failure in life, and ways to become stronger as a result of those failures.

CHAPTER 5

QUESTIONS AND ANSWERS

Q I like the concept of being 'present' with someone. Does this mean that we no longer need to buy presents for people we care about?

A Not at all. By all means, please still go-ahead and buy the presents – I certainly enjoy giving and receiving them. The statement is just a reminder that your time spent with people that you care about is also a gift.

Q There are some family and friends with whom I have kept in touch for many years. Are you saying that because I have changed as an individual, I should no longer associate with them?

A I get this question a lot. My simple response without knowing any of the detail, is for you to assess how you feel when you are with these people. Does their company and conversation make you feel valued and energized, or do you feel like time drags, and all you want to do is go home instead of being in their company. If the latter holds true, then maybe this is a sign that you should start reducing the time you spend with these individuals.

Q I like the concept of separating the person from the behavior. I just don't have the patience to deal with people like this.

A Find the patience. Call a time-out. Walk away from the situation before you say something hurtful to them. Put yourself in their shoes and consider what is driving their behavior. If you have to call them out on their bad attitude, use more 'I' statements to express how you feel. For example, say: "I felt hurt when you said that about …." Nobody can get defensive when you express the situation from your perspective. They can, however, slide into attack and blame mode if you have more 'You' in the statement. For instance: "Whenever you do this, you just think about yourself. You are very selfish..." Hopefully, by expressing how you feel, the other person will open up and tell you what is going on, so that you can uncover the real reason behind their behavior. Remember not to push a person to confide in you. When they are ready to share, they will let you know.

💬 Closing affirmations

1. There are mentors all around me, helping me through my journey in life.
2. The more I volunteer my services to others, the more I receive in return.
3. I dedicate and spend time with the people I love.
4. I tell people how much I care about them. I do this often.
5. I associate with like-minded individuals.

TAKE ACTION
CHAPTER 5 ACTIVITIES

Commitment

Observe

Nest

Tactics

Re-enforcement

Opposition

Life

Activity 1: *Engage in acts of selflessness*

Help someone achieve their goals

Look out for opportunities to help someone achieve their goals. Share a story with them to help boost their morale. Offer advice to assist them with a problem. Refer them to someone in your network who could help them. Offer to be their mentor.

Work with volunteer organizations

There is a volunteer organization out there that needs your help. Your role is to find the time and sign up. Your function as a volunteer within a non-profit organization would be maximized if you could align the values of the non-profit organization with your personal values. Below are some examples:
- If you are a professional accountant, consider joining your local accounting body and volunteer your services in one of their many committees.
- If you love working with children, consider offering your help at a children's home or orphanage.
- If you enjoy working with the elderly, there are many old-age homes and retirement villages that would appreciate your help.

When you volunteer your assistance to organizations in need, it gives you a different perspective on your own life. You will also meet other people who will in turn help you in some way. Offering your services has a way of returning the favor to you.

Give away unused items

Periodically review unused items in your house and give them away to someone else who would put them to use.

The easiest place to start is with your clothing. Review your closet. Set aside items that you have not worn in years; that no longer fit you or no longer suit your lifestyle today. If you are one of those people who keeps a stack of clothing for 'one day' when you lose weight, put those clothes in a box with an expiry date. If you do not lose the weight by that date, give away that box of clothing.

Include books, toys, furniture and ornamental items that have been accumulated for the sake of accumulation. If it does not serve a functional or sentimental purpose, give it away to someone who will put it to use.

Volunteer your assistance at work

At work, volunteer to either be a team member or to lead teams on more challenging assignments.

The benefits of volunteering for more work are listed below.
- You will increase your skill set and knowledge, as you are exposed to work with which you would not usually be involved.
- You will develop your leadership skills, if you are a project leader.
- If the project outcomes are unrelated to your current job responsibilities, you have an opportunity to demonstrate talents that might otherwise have gone unnoticed.
- Should an opportunity arise for a full-time position involving the work that you have volunteered your services for, this would put you ahead of other candidates, because you will have prior experience with those responsibilities.

■ Activity 2: *How to find your mentor*

Make a list of the top three goals you wish to achieve in the next 6 to 12 months. Think of the people who would make ideal mentors: People who would offer you advice, guidance and support as you pursue your goals.

Consider having more than one mentor at any point in time. Each mentor gives you a different perspective on the same situation. Thank your mentors for their continued support, and respect their time.

Create a list of successful people you would like to meet. Review this list every day. Find a way to personally meet with them. Take them out for lunch or coffee to have a discussion on their path to success. If it is not possible to personally meet with these people, perhaps read their biography (if the person is a celebrity), or follow their discussion groups on social media. By associating yourself with like-minded, successful people, you will be inspired to continue with your goals and to work harder to achieve your dreams.

Diversify your list of mentors and pick people from different areas of life. The more diversified your mentor mastermind team is, the more diversified your own thinking becomes.

Follow up on people's offers to help. Mentors come into your life when you least expect it. You might meet someone at a random event who could then end up becoming your next mentor. When you meet people randomly, ask yourself: "What was I meant to learn from this person?"

Finally, when mentors openly ask you to engage with them through meetings, phone calls or other forms of communication, take them up on their offers. Very often, people fail to stay in touch and they lose out on the invaluable advice a mentor could offer.

■ Activity 3: *Travel and enhance your world view*

Travel to a different city. It does not matter if it is a local or international destination, as long as it is a new environment.

Immerse yourself in the history of the place. Become fascinated with the culture and background of the people inhabiting the area. Indulge yourself in the culinary delights of the city.

Meet people and have sincere conversations. The more you do this, the more you will realize that in spite of our perceived differences, there are more elements that connect us as human beings than divide us. This realization increases your ability to connect with diversity.

■ Activity 4: *Perform random acts of Seva*

There are many volunteer organizations to whom you can offer your support. Apart from serving in formal volunteer groups, you can offer your help and service to other people in small ways too.

1. Offer a sincere and heartfelt compliment to someone. This could be a family member, friend, work colleague or total stranger.
2. Be a good listener. Sometimes people just need someone to listen to their challenge or problem.
3. Offer simple and practical advice to the person who vented their frustration with you. There is a reason why they chose to vent with you – you have some advice to offer them.
4. Lighten the mood. Fun, games and humor help people to think creatively and feel good about life.
5. Take the time to share a meal with someone. Many people eat on the go or alone. Companionship is one of the simplest gifts you can share.

■ **Activity 5:** *Look after something living*

Maintaining relationships requires constant dedication, patience and the ability to learn. If you are not in a relationship yet, start by buying a plant. Nurture it and watch it grow. If you succeed at this, then get more plants.

If you have a garden, get a bird-feeder and practice consistently putting out bird seed or fruit for the birds in your garden.

If you are ready for more commitment, get a pet and become the best pet-owner you know. Love your pet unconditionally.

You will attract a relationship with a partner in your life when you are mentally ready for it. You will attract someone who complements you as an individual, but who is also your complete opposite. Embrace the relationship. Love is unconditional and should not be questioned. People come into your life for a reason. As long as you are together, be the best 'you' in that relationship.

Accept that all living relationships eventually come to an end. People do grow apart from each other; and break-ups, divorces, and death are a reality. With a healthy perspective on life, you will have a healthy perspective on relationship endings.

■ **Activity 6:** *Make the first contact*

Think of someone you haven't heard from for a long period of time. Most people wait for the other party to make the first contact. Be the person to reach out and call them first. Life is too short to be waiting around for someone else to make the first move.

■ **Activity 7:** *Write thank-you letters*

Take the time to tell people how much they mean to you. Life is short. Do not wait to realize what a person means to you when it is too late.

Instead of writing fantastic eulogies, provide people with living testimonials. Write thank-you letters to people who are making, or have made, a significant contribution to your life.

SIX

CREATING AWARENESS
OPPOSITION

> *There is no such thing as a failed experiment; only experiments with unexpected outcomes.*
>
> ANON

Make failure your friend

We live in a world of duality, where positive and negative events, circumstances and experiences exist to help us grow. You will have darkness and light; happiness and sorrow; success and failure. If we know and accept that failure leads to success, why, then, do most people find it so difficult to deal with failure?

There are countless examples of how people, companies and countries became powerful forces once they were able to overcome their failures. If we know and acknowledge that failure is a natural part of life, why are we so afraid of it?

I believe that fear of failure can be narrowed down to two factors:
1. The manner in which you label failure; and
2. Your attitude towards failure.

Refer to Chapter Activity 1: "Find the teachings in failure."

Labeling failure

It is human nature to want to be associated with something that is good and positive, rather than something that is bad and negative. The general consensus of society is that failure is bad. If you fail at something, then everyone treats you differently. If not corrected, failure can limit your life opportunities. Failure can also be costly to fix. It is no wonder that no one wants to fail. However, at some point, we will all experience failure on some level in life.

The best way to deal with failure is to embrace the title. If people call you a failure, respond by saying, "Yes, I did fail. I am learning from my mistake and I'm working to fix things." For as long as you do not own your failure, people will constantly remind you of the fact that you failed. It is like having an invisible button on your forehead that reads: "Push me!" But, once people see that you have no qualms about owning up to your failure, they will leave you alone.

Humility and help

When you humble yourself and acknowledge your failure, people are more willing to help you get through it. If you behave smugly about the incident and act like you know it all, they will leave you to it, and watch from the sidelines.

The most powerful action that you can take is to seek help from your network of family and friends and say: "I messed up, I failed at this. Please help me through this." Using this approach, you are guaranteed to attract people with a boundless amount of advice and solutions.

You are not alone in your situation. Ask for help, and help will present itself to you. Conversely, nobody wants to help an obnoxious, egotistical, know-it-all – so do not be this person. In times of failure, humility attracts the support you need.

Shame and embarrassment

Most people are not willing to share the challenges and hardships they are experiencing for fear of being judged as inadequate, or not able to perform the job. It is easier for some people to suffer in silence than to acknowledge their weaknesses. In one of my workshops, I conduct a session in which I get my delegates to help each other through a work and personal challenge that they are trying to solve at that time. It always amazes me how, in a relatively small group of people, there are so many individuals who share common challenges. Equally, there are people in the group who have been through similar challenges and are able to offer advice or solutions.

Life experiences are universal. I believe that there is someone out in the world who has been through a similar failure you are going through now. It is your role to find those individuals and learn from them. If they can get through their challenging situation, so can you.

Limiting beliefs that oppress

I once coached a manager in her mid-30s. She expressed her frustrations to me about her challenging work situation. The words she used were: *"In my world, failure is not an option."*

I found this statement intriguing and probed a bit further as to why she felt so strongly about failure in this manner. I found out that when she was in university, she had received a bursary from a top company. In order to secure funding for her full-time, four-year degree, she had needed to pass all her subjects in the minimum time period. In order to motivate herself at the time to pass her examinations and not lose the bursary, she used to tell herself: "Failure is not an option."

I can fully understand how that statement would keep her focused on her studies, but 15 years after graduating, working in a middle management role, she still held the same belief. This created immense stress for her. In her position she needs to deal with failure on an ongoing basis. It is like trying to access a CD file on a computer that accepts only flash drives. She was trying to deal with her current challenges using old and outdated tools. What was needed was for her to update her beliefs to suit her current reality.

If you are battling to accept and embrace failure, you, too, need to assess your beliefs about failure. Become aware of old and outdated beliefs about failure that will limit your growth, and replace them with empowering belief statements. We covered how to do this within Chapter 2 activities called "Change your negative beliefs into affirmations." In her example, we rephrased her belief on failure to be: *"My lessons on failure help me to be a stronger leader in business."*

Assess your attitude to failure

> *Brick walls are there for a reason. They are not there to keep us out. Brick walls are there to remind ourselves of how badly we really want something.*
>
> **RANDY PAUSCH**

Failing is like a life test. Success is rewarded to those people who trust their instincts and have the courage to try again after learning from their mistakes. Life rewards those few individuals who endure the pain, embarrassment, and hardship for the long haul. These individuals have grit. They are the tough ones who show that they will do what it takes to get something done.

When you fail, do you focus on how bad your situation is, or do you focus on the solution? Your attitude to failure can be controlled by either your emotional or your rational mind. I spoke about how to identify and control your thoughts within the Chapter on Tactics.

When you experience failure, ask yourself quality questions, or repeat empowering statements to yourself that help you to find solutions. Here are some examples:

- What am I doing wrong in this situation?
- Why have I attracted this challenge?
- What can I learn from this experience?
- What can I do differently next time?
- Who can help me through this?
- There is a solution to this challenge and I am going to find it.

Make peace with imperfection

There is no such thing as 'perfect'. Do not try to be perfect or, guaranteed, you will be a very unhappy person. Life is about acknowledging imperfections, assessing what went wrong, and then learning from the experience.

Product and service companies know this principle well. That is why they constantly offer new versions of products and upgraded service offerings. You can learn from these companies and apply the same principle to your life. To improve on something, you first need to *try*.

Not trying is failure.

Stagnation is failure.

Giving up is failure.

Success is about living your life and trying. Make mistakes. Learn from your failures. Enjoy the journey.

Refer to Chapter Activity 2: "Predictable failure."

The importance of hope

In times of catastrophe, like floods, earthquakes, and violent storms, stories of hope and survival emerge: People, children and babies who were able to stay alive despite all odds. Be inspired when you learn of these stories. When interviewed, most of these survivors or the family of the survivors speak about hope that got them through or helped them find their loved ones.

Hope is that feeling that things will get better. It is what keeps you going. As long as you have hope, you have a strong belief that there is a way forward and that you will have another opportunity at life.

Hope is like that constant breeze that keeps the flicker of life alive. You do not serve your life by snuffing out hope when possibility still exists.

As long as you believe there is a way, you will find it. Hope is your tool to correct your failure.

Tough love

Your greatest teachers and life supporters are those who are tough on you. They are the people who point out your mistakes and tell you what you can do differently. Their approach; the tone that they adopt with you; and the manner in which they treat you might be hard to accept. You might even start thinking that they hate you. This is love in disguise.

If they really hated you, they would ignore you and leave you alone. The fact that they are spending so much time providing you with feedback aimed at helping you grow and develop means that they care for you. I would be more concerned if I was failing at life and people around me did and said nothing. That would mean they had given up on me.

Be grateful for your tough teachers. As long as you are surrounded by tough love, someone still believes in your ability and wishes for you to succeed. You might not like them right now, but one day you will thank them.

Darkness and light

I once had a discussion with a close friend who was going through a tough time.

At some point he made the following comment:

"I was walking home, thinking about my situation and what I needed to do. As I was walking, the lights of the nearby building went off, and I

was left walking in the darkness. I looked at the path ahead and realized that, in the darkness, even my shadow left me."

It was clear that he felt very alone in the situation he was faced with.

I thought about what he had said. A few days later, I received a morning message from one of my social media groups. It was about faith: "Faith is like a small lamp in a dark forest. It does not show everything at once, but gives enough light for the next step to be safe."

I forwarded that message to my friend and said: "You might not have been able to see your shadow in the darkness that night, but know you were still surrounded by 'light'. This light, called 'faith,' keeps you moving forward."

In your moment of darkness, know that you are also guided by light.

Refer to Chapter Activity 3: "Gain different viewpoints."

We have come a long way together on this journey of exploring the concepts of a contract with yourself. In the last chapter, I explore the concept of life, and explore the beliefs, assumptions and attitudes that could fundamentally shift how you live your life.

CHAPTER 6
QUESTIONS AND ANSWERS

Q **How do I get over the shame of my failure?**

A Simply by speaking to other people. The more you speak to other people, the more you will realize that other people go through similar failures, too. Knowing that you are not the only person 'failing' and that what you are going through is 'normal', helps you to lift the stigma of the failure and to overcome the shame.

Q **I was raised to be strong, and I was told that I should not show my emotions. I need to be tough for the rest of my family. So, as an adult, at times I find it hard to admit when I am wrong and to ask for help. I feel I need to be strong and deal with my own problems. This is how I grew up – I dealt with my own problems.**

A In Chapter 2 we explored the power of being aware of your current reality and that 'awareness precedes greatness'. I also explored how the beliefs and assumptions that might have held true for you in the past do not have to be the same beliefs and assumptions that you maintain today. Once you change the belief: "It is hard for me to admit I am wrong," to perhaps: "I am humble enough to ask for help," you open yourself up to other people guiding you. Strength is also about being humble enough to admit when you are wrong.

Q **It can sometimes be so hard to sustain hope in life's extreme dark moments and in failure How do you keep hope alive?**

A I maintain my inspirational journal and vision board. In Chapter 2, under the activity section, I explain how you can create an inspirational journal for yourself. In the final chapter activity, I talk about how to create a vision board. Those two tools help me to sustain hope. The inspirational journal is a reading exercise and helps me keep facts in perspective, and the vision board is a visual stimulation that reminds me of my big goals that still need to be achieved.

💬 Closing affirmations

1. Perseverance, humility and failure are my friends on my journey in life.
2. Failure is the lifeblood of my success.
3. Failure is a feedback mechanism. It is telling me to try a different approach.
4. Failure is success in disguise.
5. I welcome challenges: I am a solution-seeker.

TAKE ACTION
CHAPTER 6 ACTIVITIES

Commitment

Observe

Nest

Tactics

Re-enforcement

Opposition

Life

■ Activity 1: *Find the teachings in failure*

Make a list of your current and past failures.
Write down the lessons you have learned from them.
Reflect on how these experiences have shaped your character and made you the person you are today.

■ Activity 2: *Predictable failure*

There is a concept in engineering known as 'predictable failure'. When designing something, engineers ask the question: "If this failed, where would I predict the failure to occur." Steps are then taken to ensure that safety measures are put in place to avoid a catastrophe.

You can use this principle by asking yourself: "Where do I predict things will go wrong?" Put measures in place to limit the failure, or have back-up plans if things do go wrong. This helps to soften the impact.

■ Activity 3: *Gain different viewpoints*

When you are trying to find new ways to solve challenges and get through your failures, diversify your viewpoint. Read articles, magazines and books that offer alternative views. Watch online speeches and inspirational clips. Share your challenging circumstance with as many people as you are comfortable doing so. Become fascinated with divergent viewpoints.

Take some time to consider all the views and then decide on an action plan. Your decision should be a balance between contrarian and conformist views. Contrarian views are those that you initially do not agree on, but you can understand their merits. Conformist views are those that the majority agree on.

SEVEN

CREATING AWARENESS
LIFE

> *Change and growth take place when a person has risked himself and dares to become involved with experimenting with his own life.*
>
> **HERBERT OTTO**

$L = T - x$

It is usually only once a person has experienced losing someone very close to them that they then look at life, death, and time very differently. I should know, as I experienced it after my father passed on. In the period of mourning, I recall looking at pictures of recent holidays and times spent together. Upon looking at those pictures, I could not help thinking: "This picture was taken one year before the date of death"; "This picture was taken four months before the date of death"; and "This picture was taken three weeks prior to the date of death."

Time had suddenly taken on a new reality. I know we all talk about time being 'precious' and 'fleeting', but death has a way of making you truly feel what this means. You cannot turn back time, you can only make the best out of the time you have left.

The problem is that for most of us, our own date of death is an unknown – how much time do you have left in this lifetime?

Being the numbers person that I am, I started to wonder about what a life formula would look like, a formula that would provide you with an indication of how much time you have left to live. I came up with the following:

$L = T - x$; where:

T = The date and time of your death;

x = The days, hours, minutes and seconds already passed;

L = Amount of time left in this lifetime.

What you are left with looks like a count-down clock expressed in years; months; days; hours; minutes and seconds.

Acknowledge your gifts

Okay, I will be the first to admit that to think of your life in terms of a formula and a count-down clock against you is pretty depressing. I merely want to highlight that time is one of your biggest gifts and blessings in life.

Just as time is a gift in your life, you have a gift to offer to other people, and you have a certain 'time' in this life to discover these gifts and then to share them.

A precious stone, like a diamond, develops as a result of its tough external environment. You, too, have developed and are the person you are today as a result of overcoming certain tough external challenges.

You are unique, like a diamond.

The lessons you have learned about life in order to get to where you are today are your gift. Your gift takes the form of your skill, your experience, your insight, or your solution that you have come up with in order to achieve what you have done.

Once you identify and are clear on what your gifts are, you can live in a way that enables you to share your gifts over the course of your life.

Refer to Chapter Activity 1: "Acknowledge your gifts."

Defining your essence

Cultures throughout the world treat the dead differently. In spite of these differences, there is usually one common thread: Family burials or cremations take place where the dead called home. This gives the family a sense of comfort in a time of need: That the dead have been brought back to the place of their roots. If you are looking at a tombstone, or conducting a memorial service days or years after your loved ones have passed on, this time of reflection is a form of 'life after death'. The memory of your loved one continues to guide you, even though their life on Earth has ended.

In almost every culture, the religious belief is that when you die, the soul lives on – the essence of who you are is eternal. It is this essence that lives on in the memories of those you leave behind. Your principles; beliefs; values; and teachings get passed down to your family and friends.

Which brings me to a discussion on what does 'accomplishment' mean to you?

For most people, accomplishment means getting a shiny new vehicle; earning lots of money; receiving a promotion; or owning a lavish home in an upmarket neighborhood. While it is very admirable that you have achieved these things, they are all examples of external measures of accomplishment.

Redefine what accomplishment means to you and make it more internal – something that you can do, feel, or express to other people on a daily basis.

For example: Being able to share your knowledge in a meaningful way, or showing patience; having understanding; or expressing your appreciation and gratitude to people you care about. I am trying to highlight to you that determining your essence usually has little to do with materialistic accomplishments and more to do with how people remember you.

You cannot live forever, but the essence of your soul lives on, so it is worth considering how you would like to be remembered.

What is your 'why'?

In the movie, *Collateral Beauty*, Will Smith plays the role of a man who is trying to cope with the untimely death of his young daughter.

He does this by writing letters to time, death, and love. It is a film that leaves you thinking about how you spend time; it challenges your perspective on death, and questions how you choose to love.

What follows is a quote from the movie:

"...Love. Time. Death. Now these three abstractions connect every single human being on Earth. Everything that we covet, everything that we fear not having, everything that we ultimately end up buying is because at the end of the day, we long for love, we wish we had more time, and we fear death..."

What I gain from this quote is that we cannot change time – time is time; and we cannot change the fact that we are going to die. You can, however, **change how you love in the time you have left**, and this is about living your life with meaning that helps you develop the **essence** of how you will be remembered.

Finding meaning

In life, we all spend time on things that are both meaningful and not meaningful in the long term. For example, partying all night and over-indulging in alcohol and food might have been fun, but in the longer term these activities have not added value to your life.

Life purpose is about thinking of the time you have left and how you will use that time for high-priority activities that will add value to your essence and your legacy.

When you become clear on your life purpose, you also have a deeper appreciation for how you spend your time and who you spend your time with.

The person you were in the past is not who you have to be today. Life is about growth and development. As you experience life and become more educated, you gain knowledge and wisdom. That wisdom then changes your habits, actions and the decisions that you take. If you have made fundamental changes in your life over a period of time, people will say: "You are a different person." They would be right for saying so.

When you spend more of your time on activities that impact, influence and are of service to other people, then you are in the league of living your life with purpose.

Refer to Chapter Activity 2: "Defining your life purpose."

Is work-life balance a myth?

Time is time. Your body needs a set amount of time to rest, reset and rejuvenate. You cannot gain more hours in a day. You can adjust your schedule and organize your day in direct relation to your value system. If family is important to you, you will allocate more time to family. If community service is important to you, you will spend more time volunteering your services.

Your hierarchy of values is constantly shifting as your priorities and outlook on life change.

I believe that work-life balance is a myth.

Instead, I would like to suggest having 'life-balance'. When you have life-balance, you will balance your waking hours in alignment to your hierarchy of values. Your life encompasses more than just work. You have six other areas of life to consider: Health, wealth, social, education, spirituality and family. Try not to restrict your outlook on life with limiting labels. Broaden your definition of 'balance' and you will experience more of life.

Refer to Chapter Activity 3: "Create your vision board."

The 24-hour rule

Since time is fleeting and life is unpredictable, live your life with a 24-hour rule. If you are upset with someone, feel upset and be angry, but place a time limit of 24 hours to reconcile with that person. Waking up with grudges and ill feelings is a waste of time. These feelings weigh you down and are a negative influence at the start of your day.

My belief is that if the Earth has rotated on its axis and brought the blessing of a new day with it, I am going to move in the same direction and not be stuck in the past.

Remember that the purpose of life is not for it to get easier. Rather, it is about learning how to get better at dealing with greater levels of complexity. The most successful people in the world have achieved success because they have solved complex problems. Holding on to grudges takes away valuable mental energy that could be better utilized serving yourself and others.

Live 'new day' resolutions

There are many people who wait for a new year before making changes in their lives. Most people start counting down the year from September onwards. These are the people who cannot wait for the year to end so that they can start afresh.

I find this to be a lost opportunity. You have the opportunity of time to live your life with purpose, yet a choice is being made to count down the year to a new one.

A new year is simply a calendar shift; yet we experience a calendar shift every single day. Despite the challenges and tough days you may be experiencing, with the blessing of sleep and rest, you can wake up to a new day and experience it as you would a new year. How you treat a new day can be the same experience as how you treat a new year. Your perception and experience of life begins in your mind.

Do not wait for a new year to instill a change in your life.

Do not count down to the start of a new year to write new year resolutions.

And, certainly do not wait for a new year to feel inspired.

Every day you have the opportunity to celebrate time, just as you would celebrate the change-over of a new year. This is because, every day when you wake up, you are able to exert **C.O.N.T.R.O.L.** over your life by:

1. Reminding yourself of the **commitment** that you made in the form of short-term and long-term goals.
2. **Observing** and being aware of your life situation; being accountable; and believing in your ability to deal with whatever challenges you face.
3. Pushing yourself outside of your **nest** and getting out of your comfort zone. Every time you do this, you grow as an individual.
4. Applying a new set of **tactics** to consciously change your thinking to deal with any circumstance.
5. Reminding yourself to show gratitude and appreciation to every person who shares your life. This **re-enforces** your relationship with your network of family, friends and colleagues.
6. Having a healthy relationship with **opposition** and embracing every failure as a learning opportunity.
7. Focusing on and being present in the **life** you are living right now.

It is for these seven reasons that I believe in implementing 'new day resolutions'. You have the ability to implement change 365 days a year.

Live an inspired life, guided by your purpose and fueled by your passion. May your new day resolutions bring you clarity of thought and a new perspective on this journey we call life.

CHAPTER 7

QUESTIONS AND ANSWERS

Q Once I have completed the 'Life Purpose Statement' activity, does this mean that I am stuck with that statement and can never change it?

A Your life purpose statement was written at a time when you had particular experiences, skills and a certain outlook on life. Over time, these will change and you will grow and mature as a person. It is common practice for your life purpose statement to evolve and become refined over time. This is why you need to constantly review, adjust and assess your Life Purpose Statement.

Q I understand and agree that it is good to have a '24-hour rule' and to not stay angry for too long. However, sometimes emotional blackmail helps me get what I want faster.

A I guess we have all used emotional blackmail in some form or another for personal gain. I refer back to the chapter on 're-enforcement' and why relationships with other people are so important. Emotional blackmail is false and misleading. It manipulates people. In the long term, others might not trust your intention and may not be willing to help you. Emotional blackmail has a time limit on its use. Build your success based on your relationship with other people using respect, openness and honesty as your foundation.

Q Okay, so I admit that new day resolutions are more beneficial to my life than setting new year resolutions, but does this mean that I should not participate in new year celebrations?

A No, that is not what I am saying. By all means participate in new year celebrations – responsibly. What I am specifically referring to is the **attitude** and **mindset** that a new year resolution brings upon a person. It can create a mindset that you can only implement change once a year. I fundamentally disagree with that. You know that this mindset has been created, because you hear people say, "I cannot wait for this year to be over so that I can start afresh next year."

In contrast, when you learn to set new day resolutions, you start to cultivate an attitude that you can instill change in your life at any time of the year – you do not have to wait for a new year to do so. Knowing that you have the **choice, ability, and power, to instill change at any time you choose to** is inspiring indeed!

🗨 Closing affirmations

1. I have a purpose in life. My purpose is clearly defined.
2. I am in control of my life. I live my life to its full potential.
3. I do what it takes to reach my goals and to live the life of my dreams.
4. I am the creator of all the events and experiences in my life.
5. I am receptive to receiving feedback from all around me.
6. I set and live by my 'new day resolutions'. I am inspired.
7. I use the gift of time to share my unique gifts with other people.

TAKE ACTION
CHAPTER 7 ACTIVITIES

Commitment

Observe

Nest

Tactics

Re-enforcement

Opposition

Life

■ **Activity 1:** *Acknowledge your gifts*

You have unique gifts that are aligned to your life purpose. When you gain clarity on your gifts, you gain clarity on your life purpose.

General questions:

1. What do you have a passion for?
2. Where do you have a unique perspective?
3. What types of people do you particularly care about?
4. What are your accomplishments to date? What have you learned about yourself as a result of those accomplishments?
5. What challenges or struggles have you overcome in your life so far?
6. As a result of overcoming these challenges or struggles, what lessons have you learned?

Specific questions:

1. List five things that you have learned about yourself and achieving your dreams.
2. List five things that you have learned about working in teams.
3. List five things that you have learned about managing money.
4. List five things that you have learned about running a business.
5. List five things that you have learned about keeping a family together.
6. List five things that you have learned about religion.
7. List five things that you have learned about spirituality.
8. List five things that you have learned about being a partner in a relationship.
9. List five things that you have learned about education.
10. List five things that you have learned about being successful in a career.
11. List five things that you have learned about being influential in society.

When answering these questions, you should start to see a trend in your answers. Review your list and write down the top five gifts that you have identified for yourself.

Now that you are aware of your own unique gifts, use your gifts and share them with other people.

■ Activity 2: *Defining your life purpose*

Suppose I told you that I was giving you $20 million today. I would be investing $10m of that money on your behalf into property that would earn you a minimum return of 10% rental income of $1m per annum, which will increase with inflation each year. What would you do with the remaining $10m?

Write down everything you would do with the balance of $10m

Now assume that 10 years have lapsed since you first received the $10m, and you have traveled the world, purchased the car and house of your dreams, and bought whatever else you desired. What would you do for the rest of your life, knowing that you have a steady income flowing from rentals?

Write down what you would do for the rest of your life

The first part of the question is there to reveal all the conscious and subconscious personal or *selfish* desires; dreams and goals that a person seeks.

The second part of the question reveals that once a person has satisfied their own personal desires, when money is no longer an obstacle, their interests usually change from being selfish to selfless. The focus changes to helping those around them.

It is in the second question that you start getting close to what your own life purpose is all about.

Life purpose statement

A **goal** can be defined as something that is *attainable, tangible,* and therefore *transitory.*

Whereas, a **purpose** can be defined as an *overarching life-path; a purpose is not something that you attain, but something that drives you and something that you carry with you for your whole life. Your purpose is your heart and soul's guiding direction for life. When you concentrate and focus fully on your purpose, you develop a crystal-clear picture of success.*

When writing your life purpose statement, you need to ensure that you include three elements:
1. **Be** – What is it you would like to be?
2. **Do** – What will you do in order to live the life you desire?
3. **Have** – As a consequence of being and doing, what will you have in your life?

Illustration of a life purpose

I, [name], hereby declare before others and myself that the purpose of my life is to **be** a master in the art of painting.

I will **do** this by learning from the greatest masters and by focusing all my energy on my artwork and distributing them in high-end galleries.

In this way, I may **have** social prestige and financial abundance, while making hundreds of people feel good every day. I will leave a legacy for others to follow while working with people I admire as artists.

Once you have written down your own Life Purpose Statement, constantly review, revise and fine-tune it. This will help you to become more focused on achieving it.

■ Activity 3: *Create your vision board*

A vision board is a fun and impactful way to quickly remind yourself which areas of your life are important to focus on within the next 6 to 12 months.

There are various ways to build your vision board. This is my preferred way as it considers all areas of life.

Divide an A3 board into seven spaces that you can then fill up with pictures from the seven areas of life. The spaces do not have to be equally split up. Below is a list of those areas of life.

1. **Career** – this would include goals for your work; your business.
2. **Finances or wealth** – consider what are your savings and financial ambitions.
3. **Education or wisdom** – consider if there are any formal or short courses you wish to study for.
4. **Spirituality or religion** – I include both here. Spirituality is more about connecting with yourself, other people and the universe. Religious goals are about pursuing specific objectives in line with your religious beliefs.
5. **Societal influence or social events** – Some people might have goals that they set towards helping society at large – like volunteering in organizations. Other people may have goals of being more social with their friends and family – goals that are more about your personal fun and entertainment.
6. **Physical fitness, health and grooming** – In this part of your life, you tend to set goals about how you look, what you eat and your general health state.
7. **Family and personal relationships** – In this section, think about the goals you wish to achieve with your immediate family and friends, and your significant other.

Now that you are aware of the different areas in life, collect a range of pictures and phrases from magazines, or find relevant pictures and phrases from the Internet that represent all areas of life and paste them on your vision board. Have fun with the process and avoid 'forcing' pictures that do not make sense to you. If a picture appeals to you and you have no idea why it appeals to you at the time, just cut it out and paste it on to your vision board, anyway. You will figure it out later. At certain points in your life you will find that there are three out of the seven areas of life that you tend to have more pictures in. That is okay – it is an indication that you are focusing on those three areas of life right now.

There are no rules as to how you paste the pictures on to your board – simply make it fun and appealing. You could even make it look pretty with different colors and ribbons.

Keep the vision board in a place where you will be able to see it each day. I would encourage you to update your vision board at least once a year. You will always use a clean new sheet of paper for subsequent vision boards, but you might want to refer to your older vision board to carry over any pictures that you still have not yet achieved.

I believe that there is a lot of power in building your vision board. Complete your first one and unleash this power for yourself.

Afterword

> *There is no scarcity of opportunity to make a living at what you love; there is only a scarcity of resolve to make it happen.*
>
> **WAYNE DYER**

We have covered many life principles, along with activities after each chapter, which should help to entrench the principles being explained.

I believe that a contract with yourself is not a destination to be reached. Rather, it is a journey of self-discovery and self-actualization. Through your life experiences, you discover your hidden strengths and gifts, and you learn to do things differently. Your life experiences help you grow and mature as an individual.

It is my hope that by now, you are inspired in some way to do things differently in your life to achieve your success.

I have shared with you many personal experiences and I am eager to hear about your personal success stories, so if you have something to share, I would love to hear about it. You can contact me at info@dineshriepillay.com

Thank you for sharing this journey with me. It has been my honor to serve you.

To your success in life.

Notes

Chapter 1: Commitment

1. Demartini, J.F. 2002, *The Breakthrough Experience*, sixth edition, Hay House, Inc, Australia.
2. Le Roux, R. & De Klerk, R. 2003, *Emotional Intelligence Workbook*, second edition, Human & Rousseau (Pty) Ltd, Cape Town.
3. Eker, T.H. 2005, *Secrets of the Millionaire Mind*, first edition, Harper Collins Publishers, New York.
4. Clason, G.S. 1988, *The Richest Man in Babylon*, first edition, New American Library, a division of Penguin Group (USA) Inc, New York.
5. Hill, N. 2004, *Think and Grow Rich*, Vermilion, first edition, an imprint of Ebury Press, United Kingdom.
6. Demartini, J.F. 2004, *How to Make One Hell of a Profit and Still get to Heaven*, second edition, Hay House. Inc, Australia.
7. Loeb, M. 1996, *Marshall Loeb's Lifetime Financial Strategies*, first edition, Little Brown and Company, Canada.
8. *I Am Bolt*, Dir: Benjamin Turner and Gabe Turner, UPHE Content Group, 2016.
9. *Running Wild with Bear Grylls: President Barack Obama*, NBC.com, Season 2, Episode 9, December 2015.

Chapter 2: Observe

1. Sharma, R.S. 1997, *The Monk who Sold his Ferrari*, second edition, 2004, HarperElement, an imprint of HarperCollins Publishers, Great Britain.

Chapter 3: Nest

1. Ericsson, A. & Pool, R. 2016, *Peak*, first edition, Vintage, London.

Chapter 4: Tactics

1. Goleman, D. 1996, *Emotional Intelligence*, first edition, Bloomsbury Publishing Plc, London.
2. Robbins, A. 1988, *Unlimited Power*, first edition, Simon & Schuster Ltd, Great Britain.
3. Kehoe, J. 1997, first edition, *Mind Power into the 21st Century*, Zoetic Inc., Canada.
4. Pinker, S. 1997, first edition, *How the Mind Works*, Penguin Books, England.
5. Pink, D.H. 2005, *A Whole New Mind*, first edition, Riverhead Books, Penguin Group, New York.
6. Murray, D.K. 2009, *Borrowing Brilliance*, first edition, Random House Business Books, Great Britain.
7. *Evan Almighty*, Dir: Tom Shadyac, Universal Pictures, June 2007.

Chapter 5: Re-Enforcement

1. Demartini, J.F. 1997, *Count your Blessings*, first edition, Element Books, USA.
2. Demartini, J.F. 2005, *You Can Have an Amazing Life in Just 60 Days*, first edition, Hay House Inc, Australia.

Chapter 6: Opposition

1. Demartini, J.F. 2007, *The Heart of Love*, first edition, Hay House Inc, Australia.

Chapter 7: Life

1. Tolle, E. 2011, *The Power of Now*, second edition, Hodder & Stoughton, United Kingdom.
2. Walsch, N.D. 1995, *Conversations with God: Book One*, first edition, Hodder and Stoughton, Great Britain.
3. Walsch, N.D. 1999, *Conversations with God: Book Two*, first edition, Hodder and Stoughton, Great Britain.
4. Walsch, N.D. 1999, *Conversations with God: Book Three*, first edition, Hodder and Stoughton, Great Britain.
5. *Collateral Beauty*, Dir: David Frankel, Warner Bros. Pictures, December 2016.

Meet the author

Sometime during 2008, I was speaking to a group of retiring accountants about life and their careers, and I had a glimpse of what my life could look like when I was their age. That vision did not appeal to me. I felt like a round peg in a square hole.

Instead, I felt a calling to fulfill a dream of starting my own business, where I could spend my days making a difference in the lives of others.

I decided to train and develop people to become inspired leaders in business.

The meeting of professional path and inner passion

I am a qualified Chartered Accountant (CA(SA)) and Fellow Chartered Management Accountant (FCMA) by profession. I am also a Distinguished Toastmaster (DTM). I sometimes refer to myself as an 'educational bean counter', since I have two sought-after accounting qualifications and have chosen a path in the field of training and development.

Now, that might sound strange to you, but my background is ideal for my work with senior managers and business executives. I understand their language, and I understand how business works. It is easy for me to create a leadership development training program tailored to their needs. It is easy for me to individually coach leaders in business.

Instead of helping a company count its numbers, I now help people become more accountable for their own lives. I believe that in order to lead others, you first need to learn how to lead yourself.

You have crossed my path for a reason

I believe that there is a reason for every person with whom I come into contact. You are reading this right now because you are one of them. You might not know that reason upfront, but once you open your heart and allow me to work with you, we can uncover that reason together, and discover the leader within you.

I believe that knowledge is power and power is a form of energy. Energy is transferable. I also believe that knowledge is a gift: A gift that should be shared with others.

I have made it my life's mission to pass on the gift of my knowledge to every person who crosses my path. I do this in the form of the speeches I deliver; the products that I develop; the training programs I facilitate; and through the individual coaching programs that I offer.

Contact me if you would like me to:
1. Deliver a speech at your next conference.
2. Develop a leadership development program for your staff.
3. Be your executive business leadership coach.

With love,
Dineshrie Pillay